THE SIEGE OF KARS, 1855

uncovered editions

Series editor: Tim Coates

Other titles in the series

uncovered editions

THE SIEGE OF KARS, 1855

DEFENCE AND CAPITULATION

REPORTED BY GENERAL WILLIAMS

∞⚬⚭⚬∞

London: The Stationery Office

Applications for reproduction should be made in writing to The Stationery Office Limited, St Crispins, Duke Street, Norwich NR3 1PD.

ISBN 0 11 702454 6

First published in 1856 as *Papers relative to Military Affairs in Asiatic Turkey, and the Defence and Capitulation of Kars.*
© Crown copyright

A CIP catalogue record for this book is available from the British Library.

Cover photograph © The National Army Museum: Colonel Sir W. Fenwick Williams. Map on page xii showing detail of the siege of Kars is adapted from the Kars and Erzerum map in *Crimea* by T. Royle (Little & Co., 1969).

Typeset by J&L Composition Ltd, Filey, North Yorkshire.

Printed in the United Kingdom for The Stationery Office by Biddles Ltd, Guildford, Surrey.
TJ1201   C30   9/00

Uncovered Editions are historic official papers which have not previously been available in a popular form. The series has been created directly from the archive of The Stationery Office in London, and the books have been chosen for the quality of their story-telling. Some subjects are familiar, but others are less well known. Each is a moment of history.

Series editor: Tim Coates

Tim Coates studied at University College, Oxford and at the University of Stirling. After working in the theatre for a number of years, he took up bookselling and became managing director, firstly of Sherratt and Hughes bookshops, and then of Waterstone's. He is known for his support for foreign literature, particularly from the Czech Republic. The idea for 'Uncovered Editions' came while searching through the bookshelves of his late father-in-law, Air Commodore Patrick Cave OBE. He is married to Bridget Cave, has two sons, and lives in London.

Tim Coates welcomes views and ideas on the Uncovered Editions series. He can be e-mailed at timcoatesbooks@yahoo.com

In 1855, while the British Army was fighting alongside the French and the Turkish armies in the Crimean War, a little-known but serious siege was taking place in the eastern corner of Turkey. The city of Kars is close to Azerbaijan in the Russian Caucasus. It is a veritable fortress set within the mountains and overlooking a gorge.

The British were giving assistance to the Turkish Army by lending experienced officers to lead garrisons and train regiments. This led to a clash of cultures, which is demonstrated in the despatches. The ways and methods of the Turkish Army were not those with which a British officer was familiar.

The purpose of the war against Russia was to prevent expansion of the Russian Empire into Bulgaria and the Balkans. However, this left the area to the east of the Black Sea open to attack. This is where Kars stands.

In reading the papers which tell the story of the siege of Kars, it is helpful to know that Lord Stratford de Redcliffe was the British ambassador in the Turkish capital of Constantinople, and James Brant was the British consul in Erzeroom. Stratford de Redcliffe's main pre-occupation was the support of the British Army before Sebastapol, with the innumerable problems of supply and medical care that had arisen. As the other title, Florence Nightingale and the Crimea, *in this series shows, he was the senior British official on hand during the calamitous use of the Turkish barrack hospital at Scutari.*

In London, the Earl of Clarendon was the Secretary of State for Foreign Affairs and Lord Panmure was the Secretary of State for War in the administration of Lord Palmerston, which was formed in February 1855.

The central character, however, is General William Fenwick Williams (1800–83), whose story should not have been so forgotten by British history.

The selected despatches begin in May 1855. General Williams arrived in Kars in September 1854, having been appointed British Military Commissioner with the Turkish Army in Asia. He soon began organising the garrison there, although his repeated requests for supplies and reinforcements were met with delay and obfuscation.

Vassif Pasha was the new Commander-in-chief of the Turkish army in Kars, who was to be advised by General Williams.

Editor's note

Please note that, for ease of reference, the order of the despatches has been changed from the original report which was published in 1856. Here the despatches have been ordered according to the date that they were written. The reader should be aware that there was often considerable delay between the sending and receiving of correspondence.

Selected glossary of archaic and military terms

acquirement	experience
admission	consent
advices	official intelligence
agio	exchange rate fee
approbation	approval
arabas	country carts
assigned	referred to
bar	bank at the mouth of a river or harbour
barbette	platform for heavy guns
Bashi-Bozouk	member of the notoriously brutal Turkish Irregulars of the 19th century
breastworks	hastily constructed fieldworks
cantonment	temporary military quarters
casus belli	justified by war
chaussée	route
Circassia	region in the northwest Russian Caucasus, on the Black Sea
circumjacent	surrounding
condign	worthy
conducing	leading
culvert	arched channel for carrying water under a road
drachm	dram
dragoman	interpreter or professional guide
driblet	trickle
échelon	formation of troops, in parallel divisions
embrasure	opening in a wall for a cannon
épaulement	sidework of a battery or fieldwork
equinoctial	equal day and night
estafette	military courier or express
exactions	oppressive demands
firman	decree
grape	shot that shatters
Horse	Cavalry
imposts	taxes
insalubrity	unhealthy conditions
invest	lay siege to
Koordistan	Kurdistan
Koords	Kurds

league	1.376 modern English miles
magazines	storehouses
malversation	corrupt administration
mudir	governor of village or canton
Muharem	the first month of the Muslim year
Mussulman	Muslim
nowise	in no way
Pasha	a title for a high-ranking member of the Turkish Army
piastre	unit of currency in former Middle East; piece of eight
picquet	picket
Porte, the	Turkish imperial government (after the Sublime Porte: the chief office of the Ottoman government at Constantinople
prefer	present (charges)
prevision	foresight, prediction
proximate	approximate
Ramazan	Ramadan
rencontre	encounter
redif	militia
redoubt	fieldwork enclosed on all sides
rescript	edict, decree
Roumelia	former Turkish province in the Balkans
sanguinary	bloody
Seraskier	the Turkish Minister for War
Seraskierat	Turkish war office at Constantinople
signal	remarkable, significant
specie	coined money
Therapia	village north of Constantinople
treat with	negotiate
tumbril	two-wheeled military cart
vali	governor of a Turkish province
vaunting	boastful
victualling	feeding
vidette	mounted sentry

Siege of Kars, context map

MAY 1855

Brigadier-General Williams to Vassif Pasha

Excellency,   *Erzeroom, May* 14, 1855

I have heard from Colonel Lake that you express some
doubt as to your powers to deal with the affair relating
to the punishment of Mustafa Pasha and the Colonel
of the Regiment of Cavalry at Toprak-Kaleh, and the
nomination of a successor to him, without a previous
reference to Constantinople. Whilst I do myself the
honour to express my regret on this point, more

especially as it was your Excellency's own proposition, it is a duty I owe to you to state that I am fully aware of the silence with which your Excellency's representations have been received at the Seraskierat, and little encouragement held out to you by the honourable reception which has greeted Shukri and Hussein Pashas.

Nevertheless, your Excellency will permit me to observe that your career, thus far, having called forth the expression of my gratitude, and the approbation of the British Government, I should infinitely regret if so favourable a moment to grapple with the greatest difficulty experienced by this army should be lost. Your Excellency will admit that, so great a distance from the capital, and clothed with the authority which you possess, it would be a matter of future mortification were you to hesitate; indeed it is on these trying occasions that the responsible functionary adds to his reputation by an unflinching exercise of power.

W. F. WILLIAMS

Brigadier-General Williams to Major Olpherts
Sir,   *Erzeroom, May* 18, 1855
This despatch will be delivered to you by Mr Kelly, interpreter of the second class, whom I have procured at Constantinople expressly to attend on any officer detached, like yourself, from my headquarters. I have received a high character of him, and trust he will fufil his duties with zeal and fidelity. I recommend him to your protection and kindness, always bearing in mind his isolated position in so remote a country.

My former despatch gave you the heads of the duties I have assigned to you, and especially referred you to my instructions to Major Teesdale relative to the duties of the outposts, and wish you, as I did him, to look more to your headquarters than to affairs of outposts; and to instil into the mind of Veli Pasha the necessity of strengthening his positions, of drilling his half-disciplined men, and also of abstaining from all provocation of the enemy which might lead to defeat—such as useless and vaunting reconnaissances.

You are now fully aware of the stuff you have to deal with, at least, as regards the Turks; and you will perfectly comprehend me. I want firmness on the part of Veli Pasha, and a vigilant look-out in his front.

W. F. WILLIAMS

Brigadier-General Williams to Vassif Pasha

Excellency,   *Erzeroom, May* 19, 1855

Colonel Lake has sent me a copy of the letter he addressed to you relative to the danger of weakening your garrison, especially after its severe attack of scurvy, by permitting the men to fast during the Ramazan. I most fully agree with Colonel Lake in the advice he has tendered your Excellency in my name, and as travellers and soldiers before the enemy are released from this religious duty, and as the safety of your soldiers depends on a steady continuance of work on the fortifications, and the utmost vigilance at night, I hope your Excellency will look with a favourable eye upon the advice I now respectfully offer for your consideration.

W. F. WILLIAMS

Brigadier-General Williams to the Earl of Clarendon
(received June 25)

My Lord,   *Erzeroom, May* 29, 1855

Since I had the honour to address your Lordship on the affairs of the army of Kars, I have exerted every effort to send forward provisions to its headquarters, and to the detachments at Toprak-Kaleh. More than 4,000 mules and horses have been dispatched through my sole exertions, independent of those in the Government employ, and now that the peasants have sown their corn and barley, the arabas of the country will be at the disposal of the Government.

I have also sent eight siege-guns to Kars, to add to those now in position there.

I received last night a communication from Colonel Lake, stating that a large Russian force, consisting of 28,000 Infantry, 7,500 Cavalry, and 64 pieces of Artillery, was assembled round Gumri, and that the Mushir had received information of the intention of the enemy to attack Kars. We have in that entrenched camp 13,900 Infantry, 1,500 Cavalry, 1,500 Artillerymen, and 42 field-pieces.

The Mushir has, therefore, sent for the troops under Mehmet Pasha, at Moossul, to come to Erzeroom, and has also directed Mustafa Pasha to quit Diarbekir and proceed to the same destination. His

Excellency has also sent to Constantinople for troops. The Mushir acquiesced in my views respecting the Ramazan fast, and the garrison is consequently enabled to labour in the fortifications, as well as to keep a vigilant look-out at night.

All the forts commanding Erzeroom being armed, they were inaugurated yesterday. Mehmed Pasha, the newly arrived Vali, at my request, sent about 3,000 armed Mussulman citizens into them during the ceremony, and I hope that in the event of an attack these men will render material assistance to the slender detachments of regular troops now stationed in them.

Major Teesdale is still encamped with the work-men at the passes leading into this plain from that of Hassan-Kaleh, and after the departure of the next post I shall rejoin the Mushir, or at an earlier day if the enemy move from their cantonment around Gumri. I have also heard from Major Olpherts (27th instant), at Toprak-Kaleh. He was using all his efforts to give me information, and keep me in communication with Veli Pasha, and also reports the march of Russian troops towards Gumri.

W. F. WILLIAMS

JUNE 1855

Brigadier-General Williams to the Earl of Clarendon
(received June 25)

(Extract)   *Pass of Dévéboyonou,*
near Erzeroom, June 3, 1855

I left Erzeroom yesterday, *en route* for Kars, which place the enemy has announced, in an order of the day, his intention to attack. The Mushir had sent for all the good troops, Cavalry, Infantry, and Artillery, of the Toprak-Kaleh detachment, which would have thrown that road, from Erivan to Erzeroom, open. I however begged his Excellency to countermand this order, and all is again as it should be on the Byazid route.

If the Russians leave Georgia to attack Kars, it would show that our spies and travellers have underrated their strength, or that they find no succour coming to us either from Trezibond or Batoom; be this as it may, I have now four months' provisions in that garrison, and I trust the Central Government and the Allies will soon prove to this remnant of an army that it is not absolutely forgotten by them.

Liva Mustafa Pasha was tried last week for drunkenness and cowardice in the battle of Injé-Dereh. A Colonel and two Majors are also compromised; and I hope this example will prove salutary at the present moment, when the enemy menace, and the timid indulge in fear of the Russians, as well as distrust in the Government who has so cruelly neglected them.

Brigadier-General Williams to the Earl of Clarendon
(received July 11)

My Lord,   *Kars, June 9*, 1855
On the day after I addressed your Lordship from Dévéboyonou, I received from Colonel Lake the confirmation of the intention of the Russians to attack this place in great force. I also got a confidential message from the Mushir proposing to abandon Kars and defend Erzeroom. I instantly wrote back to Colonel Lake to beg the Mushir to act with the utmost vigour, and pressed on and reached Kars the day before

yesterday, where I have used every endeavour to instil energy into the mind of the Mushir, and I likewise abstained from remonstrating with his Excellency on his strange proposition to abandon a place which we had been at such trouble to provision and fortify, thinking, as I do, that he feels the weight of the false step he was about to take, and is willing to act upon my suggestions.

With this impression, I have been occupied all day in stationing the troops in the various batteries, in arming and supplying those batteries with ammunition, and in addressing to each regiment words of encouragement and hope. The enemy, in force about 30,000 men of all arms, accompanied by a train and vast supplies necessary for a siege, is within four hours of us, and will, most probably, attack us tomorrow.

I have advised the Mushir to write to Mustafa Pasha, of Batoom, for 5,000 to be directed on Ardahan, and to Veli Pasha, of Toprak-Kaleh, to prepare for an instant march when he shall have received orders for it. This is all I can do in our isolated and neglected state, and I am happy to say that our garrison appears in good spirits, and promises me to do its duty.

W. F. WILLIAMS

Lord Stratford de Redcliffe to M. Pisani

Sir,   *British Embassy, June* 13, 1855

I learn from Brigadier-General Williams that the Russians appeared, when he wrote, to be meditating an attack on the army at Kars, and I fear we shall have to deplore the little or tardy attention paid to my earnest and repeated requisitions for supplies and reinforcements. Even now, at the eleventh hour, it is most desirable that all which it is in the power of the Government to do in these respects, should be done without a moment's delay. According to my last advices from General Williams, money was greatly wanted, and he presses the demand most earnestly upon me. See Fuad Pasha and the Seraskier without delay, and urge them to send off as large a sum as they can possibly spare, while they are preparing whatever may yet be forwarded in point of men and supplies. The case does really seem to be very urgent.

I learn from our Consul at Trebizond, that the Russians had made an attack on Choorooksoo, and been repulsed with loss after a sharp engagement. Has the Porte any news of this?

Now that Circassia is cleared of the Russians, why should not the old idea of uniting the army at Batoom with that of Kars be acted upon in the present emergency? Suggest this impressively. I am assured that Batoom may be held with a very small force, supposing it to have works sufficient to be relied on; but of this I am no judge.

STRATFORD DE REDCLIFFE

Brigadier-General Williams to the Earl of Clarendon (received July 11)

My Lord,   *Kars, June* 15, 1855
Since I last had the honour to address your Lordship our entrenchments have been materially strengthened

by connecting the redoubts on the heights behind the town by an épaulement, and by closing the gorges of those on the plain in front of the town. I refer your Lordship to the sketch of these works which I had the honour to forward from Erzeroom. Since Colonel Lake arrived in Kars he has shown great skill and industry in improving the defective and hastily thrown up works of last year. In the labour consequent on these efforts the troops have evinced the greatest zeal and good humour, and I can with truth assure your Lordship that I never saw works executed with greater rapidity nor in a neater manner than by our Infantry, whose discipline has been most carefully attended to by Captain Thompson.

I have entrusted the defensive works on the heights behind Kars to Major Teesdale, and those on the Karadagh to Captain Thompson; on these officers devolve the safety of the outposts by night, as well as their various duties by day: Colonel Lake taking upon himself the outposts and pickets of the works on the plain, and also occasional visits to the advanced posts, which have been placed under Baron de Schwartzenburg.

Yesterday Colonel Lake, accompanied by Dr Sandwith, who interpreted for him, was attacked at the advanced posts, those posts having been incautiously pushed forward before he arrived on the ground; the Colonel's party retired with the loss of nine men killed.

The enemy's army has been encamped since its arrival in this vicinity at the villages of Zaïm and

Akché-Kalla, at the distance of three and four hours respectively; his detachments have penetrated to Ardahan, from whence ours had been withdrawn, destroyed some entrenchments erected last year, and purchased corn; the enemy has also made an incursion into Childir, and, indeed, is master of the country lying between this and the Russian frontier as far west as he chooses to push his foraging parties.

Yesterday a large force detached by the enemy to seize Ardahan returned to camp at Zaïm, and the spies report an immediate attack on our entrenchments. Their numbers have now assumed a more probable form, and I believe 30,000 of all arms, including Irregulars, to be about the truth.

W. F. WILLIAMS

Brigadier-General Williams to the Earl of Clarendon
(received July 11)

My Lord,   *Kars, June* 17, 1855

Circumstances leading me to believe that Mehmed Pasha, the newly appointed Governor of Erzeroom, was treating with indifference the urgent demands of the Mushir for the levying of Irregular Horse, and for the forwarding of provisions to this garrison, I addressed a letter to his Excellency, a copy of which I beg to enclose for your Lordship's information. I have also written to the Chief of Agara, Sherif Bey, begging him to levy as many native Riflemen as possible, and march them on Kars.

I have also taken advantage of the good disposition evinced by the Mussulman inhabitants of this town, to enrol 800 of them, and they are now at their stations with the regular troops.

W. F. WILLIAMS

Enclosure

Brigadier-General Williams to Mehmed Pasha

Excellency,   *Kars, June* 13, 1855

You are well aware that we are very short of provisions in this garrison, and that, although we have a good supply of grain at Yenikeuy (a village 50 miles off on the road to Erzeroom), it is not in our power, under the present circumstances, to send either arabas or pack-horses to bring it this way. It has therefore been considered necessary, after due consultation, to give his Excellency Sirra Pasha full powers to make such arrangements at Yenikeuy, Erzeroom, and other places, as he may deem fitting for providing, without loss of time, this garrison with provisions, and he has been furnished with letters to the different authorities to that effect.

This army owes its present straitened circumstances in great measure to the weakness and neglect of your Excellency's predecessor, and I myself witnessed whilst in Erzeroom a marked want of activity on the part of the members of the Civil Council; but I doubt not that you, who have shown yourself a zealous officer of the State, will in this respect display more activity even than you have done as heretofore, and I hope that by doing your utmost to supply the wants of this army, you will thus afford me an opportunity of giving a favourable report of your conduct to my Government. In the meantime, I feel it my duty to tell your Excellency that since your arrival in Erzeroom not a single araba of grain has reached here from your quarter, and I earnestly beg your Excellency not to lose sight of this most important branch of the service, and also to be good enough to afford Sirra Pasha every assistance in your power.

I have seen today two despatches written by your Excellency in reply to the Mushir's request for Bashi-Bozouks, by which you make it out impossible to collect any Bashi-Bozouks at all in your vast province! I sincerely regret to have to bring to the knowledge of my Government this apparent and evident disinclination on the part of your Excellency to act up to the duties imposed on you as Civil Governor, at a time, too, when, menaced as we are by the enemy, we require the presence of a vast body of Irregular Horse to keep open our communications with our central magazines.

I advise your Excellency as a friend to consider the dangerous position in which such a refusal on your part would inevitably place this army.

W. F. WILLIAMS

Brigadier-General Williams to the Earl of Clarendon
(received July 11)

My Lord,   *Kars, June* 17, 1855

Yesterday, being the feast of the Baïram, I fully anticipated an attack, and the troops were consequently
held in readiness throughout the preceding night, and
stood to their arms before daylight.

Our advanced posts were driven in soon after
daylight, and the Russian army appeared on the
height about half-past 6 o'clock: its advanced guard
consisted of three regiments of Regular Cossacks,
supported by Artillery and rockets. The main body of
Infantry marched in three columns, flanked by three
regiments of Dragoons and supported by six batteries
of eight guns each. In the rear appeared a strong column of Reserve Infantry, then the waggons carrying,
as I have since heard, three days' provision. The whole
force could not have been less than 25,000.

Nothing could be more perfect than the handling
of the enemy's army as it advanced upon the front of
our entrenchments, formed by the line of works
called Arab Tabia, Karadagh, and Hafiz Pasha Tabia,
and facing the Gumri road. Our Cavalry pickets and
Bashi-Bozouks retired, skirmishing with the Regular
Cossacks, until within 1,000 yards of our lines, when
the enemy's Cavalry made a desperate rush, supported
by its reserves of skirmishers, and also by a Rocket
troop, to enter the camp with our outnumbered
Cavalry under Baron Schwartzenburg; but they were
instantly checked by the Artillery from Arab Tabia,
Karadagh, and Hafiz Pasha Tabia; they then fell

back upon the main body of the Russian army, which retired in the same order in which it had advanced; and after halting for a few minutes finally disappeared over the hills, and has resumed its old camping-ground at Zaïm and Akché-Kalla.

As the enemy carried off their dead we could not ascertain their loss, but it is estimated from 100 to 150; ours amounted to 6 killed and 8 wounded.

The spirit of the Turkish troops was excellent, evincing, as they did, as much readiness in the defence as they had shown in the construction of their épaulements. If the enemy had attempted to carry his original intention into execution he would, I confidently believe, have met with signal disaster.

The precautions which I have recommended the Mushir to take are in nowise slackened, and we are now preparing for an attack of the heights in the rear of the city. The labour of the officers of my staff has been incessant, and I have to record my thanks to Colonel Lake, to Major Teesdale, and Captain Thompson, and to Dr Sandwith, as well as to Messrs Churchill and Zohrab, the secretaries and interpreters, whose duties are equally arduous and fatiguing.

W. F. WILLIAMS

Brigadier-General Williams to the Earl of Clarendon
(received July 11)

My Lord,   *Kars, June* 19, 1855
I have the honour to inform your Lordship that the enemy yesterday at daylight broke up his camps at

Zaïm and Akché-Kalla, and made a flank march round our entrenched camp, and is now in great force (30,000) within an hour's march of the weakest part of our position, which he may attack at any moment.

Veli Pasha has also the enemy before him. He has been ordered to defend himself if attacked, but if the enemy's force is small, he is directed on Kupri-Keuy to defend Erzeroom.

Unfortunately we have no Irregular Cavalry either with this or the Toprak-Kaleh force. I have frequently represented to Her Majesty's Ambassador the incompetency of Ismail Pasha, the late Governor-General of Erzeroom, whose duty it was to levy this essential force; unfortunately I have received no answer to these representations, beyond a bare acknowledgment of my despatches.

The enemy has already partially interrupted our communications with Erzeroom, but I hope this despatch will reach its destination.

W. F. WILLIAMS

Brigadier-General Williams to the Earl of Clarendon
(received July 18)

My Lord,   *Kars, June* 23, 1855

The Mushir has this moment informed me that, in consequence of the enemy having intercepted the direct communications with Erzeroom, he should send off, in an hour, a courier by an indirect route. I must, therefore, in as few words as possible, detail the events which have occurred since I informed your

Lordship, on the 19th instant, that the Russian army under General Mouravieff had, by a flank march, established itself opposite our entrenched camp, at a distance of three miles.

The rain has been so heavy and incessant as to prevent the enemy from any attempt to attack our lines, but he has pushed forward large bodies of Cavalry, supported by guns, burnt the surrounding villages, and destroyed one of our small depôts of grain at Chiplaklee, eight hours on the Erzeroom Road, and probably thinking that our entrenchments are too formidable to take by a *coup de main*, he has sent to Gumri for eight heavy guns belonging to that fortress, which are now on their way to his camp.

The duties of our garrison have been most trying, in consequence of the torrents of rain, but the spirit of the troops is good.

I urgently recommend the immediate landing of troops at Trebizond, and, if the season will admit of it, strong demonstrations from Redoute-Kaleh.

W. F. WILLIAMS

Brigadier-General Williams to the Earl of Clarendon
(received July 26)

My Lord,   *Kars, June* 27, 1855
The continued rains which I reported to your Lordship in my last despatch, prevented any movement on the part of the enemy till yesterday morning, when twenty-two battalions of Infantry

and a large force of Cavalry and Artillery advanced on our lines; their right division being directed on Hafiz Pasha Tabia, and their left on Kanly Tabia; this being the weakest face of our defences. Every disposition on our part was made to receive the attack, and the spirit of the Turkish troops was firm and soldier-like; but the enemy having advanced more cautiously than he did on the former occasion, halted without the range of our guns, and, having remained long enough to make the most minute reconnaissance, retired to his camp after keeping us under arms eight hours.

The damage done by the rain to our entrenchments had previously been carefully repaired, and we have taken advantage of the inactivity of the enemy today to add considerably to the interior lines of defence.

The Russian army being master of the sur-rounding country, plunders it daily, and supplies itself with fuel by unroofing the houses of the Mussulman villages, but spares those inhabited by the Armenians.

I regret to inform your Lordship that the mail bags brought to Erzeroom by the English Tatar from Constantinople, and forwarded by the Consul, fell into the enemy's hands, so we are ignorant of what has recently taken place in Europe or the Crimea. General Mouravieff politely sent back all such private letters as were barren of public or political news.

W. F. WILLIAMS

Brigadier-General Williams to the Earl of Clarendon
(received July 26)

My Lord,   *Kars, June* 28, 1855

The Russian army quitted its camp before Kars this morning at daylight, and has marched three hours to the south-east, more effectually, I presume, to interrupt our communication with Erzeroom. The command of land transport enjoyed by the enemy is enormous, and their convoys are admirably arranged; our garrison, on the contrary, has not funds to procure arabas or country carts, even supposing that the surrounding country possessed them: we must, therefore, hold this place till the last moment, whilst the enemy is master of all without the reach of our guns; moreover, the troops, who have conducted themselves so well since General Mouravieff appeared before Kars, are 23, 27, and 28 months in arrears of pay.

The Mushir has just received a despatch by his Aide-de-camp, Feky Bey, from Mehemet Pasha, the newly appointed Seraskier, to the effect that no assistance could be expected from Constantinople, but that he would write to Mustafa Pasha, of Batoom, to send us up 5,000 men, whereas that General has recently written to me to say that he had only 3,772 regular troops, and was pressed by the enemy. The Seraskier further promises to send 15,000 purses and 500 artillerymen, from the Dardanelles, and two battalions of Infantry and four squadrons of Cavalry are the only troops which he can spare from Diarbekir and Aleppo.

To this state has the apathy and indifference of the authorities at the capital reduced its Asiatic provinces.

W. F. WILLIAMS

Brigadier-General Williams to the Earl of Clarendon
(received July 26)

My Lord,   *Kars, June* 30, 1855

The enemy yesterday detached a large force, consisting of Infantry, Cavalry, and Artillery, towards the pass leading to Yenikeuy, where we have magazines of wheat and barley. The true object of this movement cannot yet be ascertained; but the Mushir has written to Veli Pasha, who is now encamped at Kupri-Keuy and covers Erzeroom, to be on his guard, and in the event of the advance of the enemy in force, to retire to the first Erzeroom entrenchments of Dévéboyonou, and thence into the redoubts which command that city. Tahir Pasha, who recently came here to assist in the defence of Kars, goes off tonight to Erzeroom, where his experience in the management of Artillery, and his knowledge of English, will be of great value.

I trust that the authorities of Constantinople will see the necessity of sending succour to Asia, both by way of Trebizond and Batoom. We have not enough Regular Infantry to effectively man our lines, our Cavalry cannot compete for a moment with that of the enemy, and in the Land Transport Department we are deficient; the fact, moreover, of our having supplies at Yenikeuny is to be attributed to the imbecility and indifference of Ismail Pasha, the late Governor-General of Erzeroom, who was repeatedly begged by me to forward those supplies on to Kars instead of unloading them at that distant depôt.

W. F. WILLIAMS

Lord Stratford de Redcliffe to the Earl of Clarendon
(received July 11)

My Lord,   *Constantinople, June* 30, 1855

The meeting which I had previously announced to your Lordship, took place this morning at the Grand Vizier's house on the Bosphorus. In addition to his Highness, the Seraskier and Fuad Pasha were present. I was accompanied by Brigadier-General Mansfield.

We found that the Porte had received advices from Vassif Pasha, brought by an officer who had left Kars about eleven days before. Despatches from General Williams also came to hand at the moment we were entering into conference. Their latest date was the 19th instant.

It appears from both sources, that the Russians, advancing from Gumri with an amount of force varying from 20,000 to 30,000, had presented themselves before Kars; that a partial engagement of Cavalry had taken place, followed two days later by an attack, which had been repulsed, on the part of the enemy, and that the town was threatened with a siege.

I collected from the Turkish officer, that when he left the scene of action, rain was falling in torrents, the waters of the river were out, and the Russians had no choice but to encamp. It appears, from the English statements, that the defences of the fortress were deemed to be of considerable strength, that the place was provisioned for a month, and that the Turkish army may be estimated at 18,000 men.

It was clear, to all present, that whether the Russians besieged or turned Kars, the Turkish army required an effort to be made for its relief with all practicable dispatch, and that of three possible modes of acting for that purpose, the only one likely to prove effective was an expedition by Kutais into Georgia. To send reinforcements by Trebizond would be at best a palliative. To establish an entrenched camp at Redoute-Kaleh, would, at this unhealthy season, be equivalent to consigning the troops to destruction.

The real question was, whether a force, numeri-cally sufficient, and in all respects effective, could be collected in time at Kutais to make an excursion into Georgia and threaten the communications of the Russian army, placing it indeed between two hostile forces should the Turkish army still be in a condition to take the field.

It was for the Turkish Ministers to solve this prob-lem, and they proposed that the expeditionary force should be composed of 12,000 men from Batoom and the neighbouring stations; of the troops made over to General Vivian, and estimated at 10,000 of all arms; of General Beatson's Irregular Cavalry, of 10,000 men to be detached from the army in Bulgaria as the complement of the Turkish

Contingent; of 5,000 more derived from the same source; of an Egyptian regiment of horse now here, and of another regiment expected from Tunis. To these the Seraskier proposed to add 2,000 Albanians by way of riflemen. These several forces completed, according to the figures, would present a total of 44,400 men, not perhaps to be reckoned with prudence at more than 36,000 effective.

Admitting the urgency of the case, and the consequent necessity of incurring a certain degree of hazard, I called attention to the importance of not exposing the Turkish Contingent, or General Beatson's Horse, prematurely, to a trial beyond their strength. It was accordingly understood that supposing the expedition to be resolved upon, neither of these corps would be required to embark for Redoute-Kaleh until the preparations were completed in other respects; and it is to be hoped that the interval thus gained for their benefit would suffice to secure their efficiency. I took, moreover, the liberty of remarking that the proposed expedition, besides being prepared with secrecy and sanctioned by superior authority, must finally depend for its adoption on our available means of providing it with all the requisite appliances. This indispensable field of inquiry might be investigated with advantage by General Vivian, the Seraskier Pasha, and Brigadier-General Mansfield, who, indeed, have undertaken to meet tomorrow for that purpose.

The Turkish Ministers having expressed their readiness to entrust the direction of the expedition, should it eventually take place, to a British Commander, and to accept General Vivian in that capacity, subject, of course, to the approval of Her Majesty's Government, I lost no time after our separation, in communicating personally with that officer, and putting him in possession of all that had passed on the subject of our discussion.

It only remains for me at present to refer your Lordship to the accompanying memorandum, for which I am indebted to General Mansfield. It contains information resulting from inquiries addressed to the Seraskier and his colleagues on several matters, from which it is most desirable, with a view to our ultimate success, that all uncertainty should, as far as possible, be removed.

STRATFORD DE REDCLIFFE

Enclosure

Information obtained from the Seraskier with reference to the proposal of the Porte to relieve the Army of Kars by an operation from Redoute-Kaleh towards Tiflis

Questions having been put to the Seraskier, the following information was obtained:

1. The country in the neighbourhood of Redoute-Kaleh is declared to be low and marshy.
2. A sufficient supply of grain for the maintenance of an army without the importation of corn cannot be found. The country from the coast to Kutais cannot supply the necessary magazines.

3. Ships engaged in the supply of the army would seek Batoom for safe anchorage. Redoute-Kaleh is impracticable except for boats of small draught.

4. The exact distance from Redoute-Kaleh to Kutais is eighteen hours or about fifty English miles.

5. There is no coast road practicable for guns from Batoom.

6. The River Rhion is navigable by boats as far as Kutais. The necessary boats can be sent from Trebizond.

7. The streams which run into the Rhion below Kutais are not of any significance, and are not serious obstacles to the advance of an army.

8. The population of Kutais is about 10,000, rather under than over that number.

9. The climate of Kutais is more healthy than that of the coast. It is, therefore, more prudent to throw the troops forward, after their disembarkation, as quickly as possible.

10. Labourers can be secured in the country to assist the engineers in forming an entrenched camp at Redoute-Kaleh.

11. The population in the region referred to is indifferently disposed towards the Turkish Government, since the fatal affairs of last year. It would be very difficult to attract recruits to the ranks independently of raising the country on a grand scale by acting on the Chiefs.

12. The force at Batoom and in its neighbourhood is 15,000 strong, of whom 12,000 effective men can be spared for the expedition.

13. Of these 700 or 800 men are Artillerymen. There are 30 or 32 field-guns quite ready, besides some guns of position.

14. It is also said that means of land transport for the 12,000 men at Batoom are actually available.

15. It is declared that the Russians have constructed a *chaussée* [route] from Tiflis to Redoute-Kaleh, the commerce on that line having been always much favoured by them.

16. The Porte would depend upon the British and French Admirals for assistance in transporting the troops to Redoute-Kaleh. But many steamers and transports may be spared from the transport fleet engaged in supplying Omer Pasha. Besides that, the Porte is prepared to buy other transports for this purpose.

17. The Porte proposes to give the command of the army, which, when concentrated, will exceed 43,000 men of all arms, to Lieutenant-General Vivian, now in command of the Turkish Contingent. The latter would form a division of the force.

18. The details of the force cannot, however, be analysed and decided on, till a decision is made that the design shall be put into execution.

19. There are some officers attached to the Seraskier who possess a considerable local knowledge of the country alluded to, and would be placed at the disposal of Lieutenant-General Vivian.

20. The force will be composed as follows:

Vivian's Contingent	20,000
Beatson's★	3,000
Batoom Garrison	12,000
Albanians	2,000
To be drawn from Bulgaria	5,000
Regiment of Egyptian Regular Cavalry	800
Tunis Horse	600
Total	43,400

W. R. MANSFIELD
Brigadier-General

★ 3,000 men are raised. The force to be levied by Major-General Beatson, when completed, will be 4,000.

JULY 1855

Lord Stratford de Redcliffe to the Earl of Clarendon
(received July 11)

My Lord,   *Therapia, July* 1, 1855
Agreeably to what I stated in my preceding
despatch, Lieutenant-General Vivian and Brigadier-
General Mansfield waited this morning on the
Seraskier at his Excellency's office in town. Fuad
Pasha attended at the request of the Seraskier; M.
Pisani was also present.

Enclosed herewith for your Lordship's information is a memorandum containing General Mansfield's notes of what took place on that occasion. The statement promised by General Vivian can hardly reach me before tomorrow, and perhaps not in time to be forwarded by the messenger.

Your Lordship will do me the honour to bear in mind that the proposed diversion at Redoute-Kaleh originated with the Porte; that recognising the urgency of the case I have endeavoured to obviate such manifest objections as the premature employment of the Turkish Contingent, and the exposure of troops to a climate which, at this season of the year, has been characterised as pestilential on the coast of Circassia; and that I lean entirely on military opinions as to the means of eventually carrying out the proposed expedition.

I propose at the same time to reserve the approval of Her Majesty's Government, and to afford the Commanders-in-chief an opportunity of declaring their opinions.

I have to add, in conclusion, that an entrenched position at Redoute-Kaleh will probably be found indispensable as a point of retreat in case of any signal reverse; and, with a view to future questions, it may be desirable to have it clearly understood that the Turkish Contingent is to be regarded in the light of a British force, composing the principal part of the expeditionary army.

STRATFORD DE REDCLIFFE

Enclosure

Memorandum of interview between the Seraskier, Fuad Pasha, Lieutenant-General Vivian, and Brigadier-General Mansfield, on the 30th of June, 1855

The Seraskier, before the arrival of Fuad Pasha, spoke of the affairs of the Turkish Contingent under the command of Lieutenant-General Vivian. That force has now actually in camp 8,500 men, two battalions having joined this very day. The remaining 1,500 men necessary to complete the first half of the Contingent are in Constantinople ready, and will be sent to the camp forthwith.

The second half of the Contingent to be assembled at Varna. If the plan discussed at the house of Aali Pasha is decided on, the orders for them to assemble at Varna to be immediately sent. If there is no such object, the Seraskier considers a further reference must be in the first instance made to Omer Pasha, who would take offence if a large portion of the troops in Bulgaria were drafted away without his consent: but in case of the project being decided on to form an army to operate towards Georgia, of course that such a reference might be put aside, considering the urgency of the matter. Supposing the order to be sent without delay to Bulgaria, 10,000 men could be assembled and ready to be transferred to the officers deputed by General Vivian at Varna in 15 days.

On being asked what steps could be taken to form a depôt in case of the Contingent being sent on service, he replied that it was not the Turkish custom to form depôts; that the Porte raised about 18,000 or 20,000 recruits a year, who were immediately sent to the different battalions.

On the matter of arms, he declared that he was ready to supply the Contingent with 15,000 percussion muskets immediately, although he trusted that the Minié guns sent for from England by General Vivian would soon make their appearance. The percussion muskets are now in the arsenal, and there is plenty of ammunition.

Fuad Pasha having arrived, General Vivian desired that his Excellency would have the goodness to explain exactly the views of the Turkish Government on the subject of an expedition to the coast, in which it was proposed to employ him.

Fuad Pasha then, at great length, went over all the matters which had been brought forward before his Excellency Lord Stratford de Redcliffe, the day before.

He explained the situation of the army of Kars, and that it was proposed to relieve that army by a powerful diversion. That this diversion could be best made, indeed, only made, from Redoute-Kaleh, or some place in its vicinity, for the landing of troops and the establishment of a basis of operations. That troops so landing should be thrown in advance as quickly as possibly on Kutais, and operate towards Tiflis, where it is considered the real objects of a war against Russia by the allies may be best obtained. That by such a grand operation the best chance for the army of Kars is secured, whereas by any other mode means would be frittered away, without result, either immediate or ultimate, to the good of the cause. That if the project is not adopted from want of means they must have recourse to those measures in which they have no confidence. General Vivian replied that he should like to know what means were disposable for so great a plan.

Fuad Pasha answered that, in the first place, there was of the Contingent now ready, actually at Buyukdere	10,000
That part of the Contingent to be immediately assembled in Bulgaria	10,000
To be drawn in addition from the garrisons in Bulgaria, and attached to the British Contingent in camp	5,000
Beatson's Horse	3,000
Albanian Light Troops	2,000
Garrison at Batoom and in the neighbourhood	12,000
One regiment of Egyptian Regular Cavalry	800
A body of Cavalry expected immediately from Tunis	600
Total	43,400

It was proposed to give the command of their army to General Vivian himself. On being pressed as to the means of transport inland, Fuad Pasha declared that the plans once fairly decided on, every effort would be made to furnish all the means of whatever description.

General Vivian said that he begged that he might not be misunderstood. That he put himself out of the question; but that it was one thing to throw an army on a coast, and another to feed and move it. That it was necessary for him to have exact details on this matter, on which success depends altogether. Further, that he quite admitted the justice of the reasoning addressed to him, which seemed to vouch for the necessity of employing his Contingent, that there was a State necessity against which he, as a military officer, had nothing to say. But that while he admitted this he must inform the Porte that the employment of the Contingent was premature, and, as is self-evident, cannot but interfere with the arrangements and organisation he has so much at heart.

Important, however, as these considerations are, that it is his business to carry out the orders, as far as lies in his power, of the Government under which he is acting, and that his only desire is to do that as effectually as may be, according to the injunctions he may receive from Her Majesty's Ambassador. But that putting all personal considerations on one side, they cannot be too careful in arranging the necessary matters of detail, sea and land transport, provisioning and victualling, ammunition, payment, etc.

To this Fuad Effendi agreed, and proposed that General Vivian should sketch out on paper what he considered indispensable to enable this project to be carried out. That the officers of the Porte would then be able to judge whether they had the necessary means; but that there ought to be no delay. General

Vivian promised to send such a document the next day, and expressed his gratitude for the high honour which had been conferred on him.

W.R. MANSFIELD

Major Olpherts to Lord Stratford de Redcliffe
(Extract)   *Erzeroom, July* 2, 1855
I think it my duty to acquaint your Lordship with the state of affairs in this quarter up to the latest moment, lest the communications which you receive from General Williams be interrupted by the Russians, who were yesterday in force on the direct road between this and Kars, at the village of Chiplaklee, and whose advanced posts towards Erzeroom had reached Yenikeuy, a village situated on the Soghanli-Dagh range—the principal natural barrier to their rapid progress into the heart of Armenia.

I saw General Williams at Kars, on Friday evening, but only for a few minutes (having ridden in on my own responsibility), as the enemy were then moving towards Chiplaklee, and the General required my immediate return to the force under his Excellency Veli Pasha, at Kupri-Keuy. I have been with the Pasha's Division since the middle of May last, at Euch-Kelissa, on the Byazid frontier. We withdrew from this position when Kars was attacked, to our present one at Kupri-Keuy, covering Erzeroom about 25 miles behind us.

At Kars all were well, and no immediate danger apprehended for the safety of its garrison, but the intentions of the enemy are not yet apparent; their late move to the Soghanli-Dagh Passes, while it still more isolates Kars, threatens Erzeroom. I beg, therefore, most respectfully to suggest to your Excellency the necessity of urging upon the Porte the dispatch of reinforcements to Trebizond.

I write this from the house of Mr Consul Brant, to whose care, I beg, my Lord, you will kindly send any reply with which your Lordship may be pleased to favour me. My proper headquarters are with his Excellency Veli Pasha, at Kupri-Keuy. I have explained to the three Pashas in camp, and to the Pashas of the Medjlis here, my views and procedure in addressing your Excellency, and they have assured me that a similar communication has been made by them to his Excellency the Seraskier, so that I hope not a day may be lost, for the foe are all but at the very gates of this capital.

Consul Brant to Lord Stratford de Redcliffe

My Lord,   *Erzeroom, July* 3, 1855

I have the honour to inform your Excellency that I received a letter from Kars, dated 26th instant. The Russians took the post from hence, conveying the letters brought by Mazloom Tatar. General Mouravieff politely forwarded to Kars those which contained no news, and no allusions to the war; but he kept back the despatches, the newspapers, and private letters which contained news.

At 6 A.M. on the 26th, General Williams and his staff were roused by an alarm given of the advance of the Russian army. It bore down on Kars in two columns, one approaching by the Gumri road, and the other directly in the face of Kars; they halted their army at about a mile and a half or two miles from the Turkish works. At 10.30 P.M., they fired one gun, and retired to their camp. The force is said to have consisted of about twenty-two battalions.

General Williams desired the writer to tell me, in case his despatches should not reach in time for the post of the 3rd of July, to communicate the above intelligence.

His Excellency Hafiz Pasha of Trebizond is preparing a large force of Bashi-Bozouks; from the haste with which they are collected and the classes which are to contribute to swell up the number, I should think the real efficiency of the reinforcement will be small. Better to have 10,000 European soldiers than such hordes of undisciplined men.

If 10,000 good troops were quickly landed at Trebizond, and brought up here by rapid marches, easing the men by loading their knapsacks and other traps on horses, they could arrive here easily in ten days from Trebizond; such a force would suffice for defence, and other reinforcements could follow more leisurely.

Veli Pasha's division is at eleven hours' distance from hence, on the Kars road, waiting orders what direction to take, with Infantry, Cavalry, Artillery, and Bashi-Bozouks. I am told there may be about 8,000 men; but the numbers of each I am not able to state.

I send this by a return messenger from Trebizond.

JAS. BRANT

Lord Stratford de Redcliffe to the Earl of Clarendon
(received July 16)

My Lord,   *Therapia, July* 5, 1855
No information, as far as I know, has reached
Constantinople respecting the state of affairs at Kars.
My latest despatch from General Williams was dated
on the 19th ultimo. The correspondence which I forwarded to your Lordship has, no doubt, stated the
same particulars which were conveyed to me.

Enclosed herewith, in copy, is the last despatch
which I have addressed to Her Majesty's
Commissioner. It distresses me greatly that I am
unable to hold out any more immediate prospects of
relief.

STRATFORD DE REDCLIFFE

Enclosure

Lord Stratford de Redcliffe to Brigadier-General Williams
Sir,   *Therapia, June* 22, 1855
I have the honour to acknowledge the receipt of your
several despatches to the 19th ultimo; and while I
express my concern at the danger to which the
Turkish army at Kars appears to be exposed, I cannot
but admire the spirit with which you were prepared
to meet the enemy.

I have never ceased to recommend that reinforcements and supplies should be sent to Vassif Pasha; and I
hope you are persuaded that the shortcomings of the
late Seraskier are as much condemned by me as by you.

I am now engaged in concerting measures for the relief of the Turkish forces in Kars and Erzeroom; but if anything efficient can be accomplished, it must be, I fear, more or less a waste of time; and we trust that, whether the enemy stop to besiege Kars, or mask it and push on to Erzeroom, the Turkish Commander will be able, with your support, to maintain a firm position.

STRATFORD DE REDCLIFFE

Brigadier-General Williams to the Earl of Clarendon
(received July 26)

My Lord,   *Kars, July* 7, 1855

The force detached by the Russian General on the 29th ultimo in the direction of Yenikeuy, which I have already had the honour of communicating to your Lordship, consisted of 15 battalions of Infantry, 40 guns, and three regiments of Cavalry; and, as I anticipated, he destroyed our magazines of biscuit, wheat, and barley, which contained, at least, two months' supply for our garrison. The remainder of the enemy's army comprised an equal force with that of the expeditionary column, and was posted in a most commanding position, only assailable at one point, and that by a long *détour*, and out of our power to disturb, without risking the ultimate fate of our garrison.

The position occupied by Veli Pasha at Kupri-Keuy, and the fortifications recently constructed at Erzeroom, no doubt, prevented the Russian General from hazarding an attack in that direction; for his numerous and excellent Cavalry, and overpowering field artillery (80 guns), render him master of everything out of the reach of our cannon.

Yesterday the enemy returned to the camp before Kars, and his reunited forces are ready either to assault or to more closely invest us, by cutting off our only remaining communication with Erzeroom *via* Olti.

W. F. WILLIAMS

Vice-Consul Stevens to Lord Stratford de Redcliffe
My Lord,   *Trebizond, July* 9, 1855
I have the honour to report that our Pasha left for Erzeroom yesterday with 300 artillerymen and 20 field-pieces. A large force of Irregulars, which may reach the sum of 10,000, is now assembling, and will march today for the same place.

FRA. I. STEVENS

Lord Stratford de Redcliffe to the Earl of Clarendon
(received July 23)
My Lord,   *Therapia, July* 12, 1855
Conceiving that your Lordship must feel anxious to obtain as much information as possible respecting the present state of the army at Kars, I do myself the honour to enclose herewith an extract of a private letter from Erzeroom, communicated to me by a private hand, and derived from what I consider to be a reliable and well-informed source.

STRATFORD DE REDCLIFFE

Enclosure

Extract from a letter dated Erzeroom, June 26, 1855
Our letters from Kars are dated the 23rd. The Russians were then in their camp almost swamped by the rain. They sent out their horsemen, and they have full liberty to do so as they please, for the Turks have no mounted men to oppose them. They came to Chiplaklee, one station beyond Yenikeuy [villages on the road between Kars and Erzeroom] and there they destroyed some grain, and retired to their camp. They sent to Gumri for eight heavy guns to play on Kars; they stuck in the mud near Arpatchai, but horses and men were sent to get them out and bring them to their camp. It is about an hour from Kars, and the tents can be seen and counted; but they are spread over a wide space, probably to make the army appear larger; they have ascertained that their force is 24,000, among which a large proportion of Cavalry, a great part irregular. The Turkish troops are in high spirits, and the townspeople full of courage and alacrity; about 1,000 have been supplied with arms, at their own request, and come to their post on the least alarm without being sent for. The Russians will never take Kars but by a regular siege, and those within have no fears while they have ammunition; nevertheless it was indispensable to send up succours.

Lord Stratford de Redcliffe to the Earl of Clarendon
(received July 23)
My Lord,   *Therapia, July* 12, 1855
The extreme importance of obtaining correct data before the expedition proposed for the relief of the

Turkish army at Kars be finally submitted to Her Majesty's Government, produces an unavoidable delay in the progress and preparation of the plan. The Turkish Government has decided on sending confidential officers to examine the localities at Trebizond, Batoom, and Redoute-Kaleh, with a view to forming a more correct idea of their resources and difficulties. I hope that General Vivian and Sir Edmund Lyons will pursue the same course, and that an officer from each service will be sent in a suitable vessel to obtain the requisite information on the coast. I have already applied to General Vivian and Rear-Admiral Grey for the purpose, and I shall avail myself of the earliest opportunity to make a similar application to Admiral Sir Edmund Lyons.

I abstain from troubling your Lordship with particulars until I can submit the complete result of the present inquiries to Her Majesty's Government. The general nature and object of the plan entertained by the Porte, and promoted as a matter of eventual execution by Her Majesty's Embassy, has been explained to your Lordship in my preceding despatches.

STRATFORD DE REDCLIFFE

Lieutenant-Colonel Simmons to
Lieutenant-General Simpson

Sir,   *Camp near Kamara, July* 12, 1855

Omer Pasha sent to you yesterday a note in which he proposed that he should go with the 25,000 men he had brought from Eupatoria to make a diversion in favour of the garrison of Kars and the Ottoman army in Asia.

Since sending that note he has received a communication from the Government at Constantinople in which he is entreated to consider what can be done to save the interests of Turkey in Asia.

The Government inform him that if Kars should fall there is no force to prevent the Russians marching directly upon Constantinople, and it is probable that success on the part of the Russians would decide the Persians to take arms against the allies.

The Porte have proposed to General Vivian to take the Turkish Contingent there, and both Lord Stratford and General Vivian have expressed their willingness that it should go.

Omer Pasha, however, thinks that there will be great risk in sending them there, as the men are not yet acquainted with their officers; the officers do not speak their language, and consequently cannot command them in the field, and the Contingent, although it might form a garrison, cannot yet be in a condition to march into the interior. The force of the Contingent also is small to make the contemplated operation.

Omer Pasha also thinks that possessing, as he does, the confidence of the Turks, and being well known in Asia, where he has made several campaigns, he is more likely to gain the sympathies and assistance of the inhabitants in provisioning, in gaining information, etc., than strangers who do not know the language or country.

Under these circumstances, Omer Pasha thinks that it will be decidedly advisable, in the interest of the common cause, that the Contingent should be assembled at Shumla, as proposed by him, where it could be organised and made ready for the field by next spring; that he should take the whole of his force hence, and from Kertch, with Cavalry from Eupatoria, and, if necessary, an additional number of men from Bulgaria, and make the operation himself.

By threatening the communications of the Russians with Georgia, they will be obliged to abandon the siege of Kars; and the winter ensuing, all operations would be suspended until the spring of 1856, and time will thus be gained to form an army in Asia sufficient to protect the Turkish dominions on that side, which Omer Pasha confidently thinks he could do by his influence and knowledge of the country.

Omer Pasha has requested me to submit these considerations to you previous to the conference which he has requested General Pélissier to assemble.

J. L. A. SIMMONS

The Earl of Clarendon to Lord Stratford de Redcliffe
My Lord,   *Foreign Office, July* 13, 1855
The plan proposed by the Porte for the relief of the Turkish army at Kars, as sketched out in your Excellency's despatches of the 30th of June and 1st instant, has been attentively considered by Her Majesty's Government; and I have to state to your

Excellency that it appears to be objectionable for the following reasons:

It would be in the greatest degree imprudent to throw on an unwholesome coast, without means of land transport, without any certainty of provision, without an assured communication with the rear, without an accurate knowledge of the country to be traversed, or the strength of the enemy to be encountered, and with the probability of a hostile population, 40,000 men, hurriedly collected from various quarters, imperfectly disciplined, doubtfully armed and equipped, and as yet unorganised, and to expose them at once to all the hazards and difficulties of a campaign against a Russian army. They would fall ill between Redoute-Kaleh and Kutais, and be defeated between Kutais and Tiflis. Moreover, the fragments to be united for the purpose of composing this army are so scattered about, that the crisis, if it is to take place, would be over long before it could reach the scene of action.

Her Majesty's Government are of the opinion that the wiser course would be to send reinforcements to the rear of the Turkish army, instead of sending an expedition to the rear of the Russian army. The reinforcements might go to Trebizond, and be directed from thence upon Erzeroom. The distance from Trebizond to Erzeroom is less than from Redoute-Kaleh to Tiflis, and the march is through a friendly instead of through a hostile country; and at Erzeroom the army would meet supporting friends instead of opposing enemies, and supplies instead of famine.

If the army at Kars cannot maintain that position against the Russians, it should fall back upon Erzeroom, and the whole Turkish force should be concentrated there. If the Russians are to be defeated, it will be easier to defeat them by the whole force collected, than by divided portions of that force; and a defeat would be the more decisive, the further it took place within the Turkish frontier.

Trebizond is a port where supplies of all kinds might be landed; and Her Majesty's Government believe that it is a healthy place, and that Erzeroom is so likewise.

Such an arrangement as that which I have described would give time for collecting and organising the various detached corps of which the proposed army of 40,000 men is to be composed; and Her Majesty's Government entirely concur in Lieutenant-General Vivian's opinion that an army thrown on a coast without means of transport and supplies, is doomed to destruction.

CLARENDON

The Earl of Clarendon to Lord Stratford de Redcliffe
(Telegraphic)   *Foreign Office, July* 14, 1855
The plan for reinforcing the army at Kars, contained in your despatches of the 30th June and 1st instant, is disapproved. The reasons will be sent by the messenger today against employing the Turkish Contingent until it is fit for service.

Trebizond ought to be the base of operations, and if the Turkish army of Kars and Erzeroom cannot hold out at the latter place against the Russians, it might fall back on Trebizond, where it would easily be reinforced.

Lord Panmure to Lieutenant-General Vivian

Sir,   *War Department, July* 14, 1855

I transmit herewith, for your information, a copy of a despatch [dated July 13, 1855] which the Earl of Clarendon has addressed by the present opportunity to Her Majesty's Ambassador at Constantinople, on the subject of the plan proposed by the Porte for the relief of the Turkish army at Kars, and I have to acquaint you that I entirely concur in all that is said in that despatch as to the objectionable character of the plan proposed by the Porte.

I place such full reliance on your professional ability that I feel no anxiety lest you should undertake any expedition of a nature so wild and ill-digested as that contemplated by the Porte.

Whilst it is your duty to give every aid in your power, not simply as commanding the Contingent, but as a British officer enjoying the confidence of Her Majesty's Government, to our allies the Turks, it is at the same time necessary that you should be cautious in not risking the honour of the British name and your own reputation by undertaking military operations for which proper bases have not been laid down, communications opened, supplies arranged, and transport provided.

A *coup de main* by means of suddenly throwing an army on the coast to threaten, or even to attack an enemy's stronghold, is one thing; but a deliberate expedition to invade an enemy's country, and on his own territory to make war upon him, is quite another.

In the first case, something may be hazarded; but in the other, every preparation must precede action.

Moreover, from all the information which has reached me, I have every reason to believe the army of Batoom to be in a deplorable state. I know the Contingent to be scarcely organised; of the Bulgarian troops you can have no knowledge, and I presume that Beatson's Horse are as little reduced to control and discipline as your own troops. In short, I am assured that it would be madness to attempt to succour Brigadier-General Williams in this way. It is too late to regret the policy which has left that gallant officer and his army exposed to such straits; but it would only be opening the way to fresh failure to follow out such schemes as have been proposed for the purpose of relieving him. You must, as I have no doubt you feel, lose no time in getting your force into order for service, which will be sure to await you somewhere, as soon as you are ready for it; but organisation is as necessary for an army as endurance and valour, and without the former the latter qualities are utterly unavailing.

PANMURE

Brigadier-General Williams to the Earl of Clarendon
(received August 8)

My Lord,   *Kars, July* 14, 1855

Since the date of my last despatch of the 7th instant, we have diligently worked at an interior line of entrenchments on the town side, as the enemy's camp remained stationary on the hills in that direction.

On the 12th instant General Mouravieff marched three hours to the south, and encamped at the village of Boyouk-Tikmeh, leaving eight battalions, two batteries, and a regiment of cavalry to observe our garrison. I at once conceived his object to be that of attacking the southern heights above Kars, which form the key of our defences, and by the crowning of which Kars was taken in 1828. We consequently began to entrench those eminences, and the enemy made minute reconnaissances of them on the 11th and 12th instant.

Yesterday, the whole Russian army marched towards them, and the force left by the enemy on the heights in our front moved up close to Kanly Tabia to engage our attention; but we were, nevertheless, enabled by our central position so to reinforce the menaced heights, that General Mouravieff, after some hours of close reconnaissance, retired to his camp. As this visit was made with his entire army, I presume he would have assailed us if he had found such a step desirable to his future operations.

The enemy remains quiet today, but our new redoubts on those hills are pressed forward with vigour, and, indeed, enthusiasm by the troops.

I have just heard that the Russian General expects reinforcements from Byazid *via* Gumri, and that those troops, recently expelled from the garrisons of the coast of Circassia, are also marching into the interior of Georgia, and may take part in the future operations against Asia Minor.

W. F. WILLIAMS

The Earl of Clarendon to Brigadier-General Williams
Sir,   *Foreign Office, July* 18, 1855
I have great pleasure in conveying to you the cordial approbation of Her Majesty's Government for the untiring zeal and energy which you have displayed in collecting supplies, in keeping up the spirit of the Turkish army, and in placing Kars in such a state of defence that the first attack of the Russians was a signal failure.

Her Majesty's Government do not doubt that you will perservere in the same course, notwithstanding the great difficulties of every kind against which you have to contend, and they trust that your exertions will meet with the success which they so well deserve.

The Earl of Clarendon to Lord Stratford de Redcliffe
(Extract)   *Foreign Office, July* 19, 1855
I have received your Excellency's despatch of the 6th of July, reporting that most of the articles required have been sent to the army at Kars by the Porte, and I have to state to you the Her Majesty's Government fear that the succour will arrive too late.

Brigadier-General Williams to the Earl of Clarendon
(received August 20)

My Lord,   *Kars, July* 21, 1855

From the date of my last despatch on the 14th up to
the present time, the Russian army has remained in the
camps occupied by it prior to the third demonstration
made by General Mouravieff against our entrenched
positions. His powerful Cavalry, however, has not been
inactive, having blocked up the roads leading from this
to Erzeroom, *via* Olti, and also the one to Ardahan, by
which we received our scanty supply of barley.
Fortunately we have in store nearly three months' supplies of biscuit, flour, and wheat; we therefore may
hope to be relieved before this amount of food is con-
sumed. Any reinforcements sent by the Turks, from
whatever quarter they may be, must come with convoys of provisions; otherwise, such accessories of force
would amount to positive loss to the chances we now
feel of holding out until the allied Governments, by
wise combinations and sufficient forces, can oblige the
Russian army to retire into Georgia.

There is a report in circulation relative to the
Russian troops recently expelled from the forts in the
Black Sea which causes us anxiety, namely, that several
battalions of them have reached Tiflis; it is, however,
added "in great disorder"; but such is the discipline of
the Russian army, that these bands may soon be reor-
ganised and added to General Mouravieff's forces
now before us.

The Russian General has now minutely and
closely observed our positions. As he marched round

us, we have anticipated his arrival at the menaced point, by adding to and increasing the strength of our defences, at which the Turkish Infantry work with cheerfulness and surprising tact and intelligence.

W. F. WILLIAMS

Lord Stratford de Redcliffe to the Earl of Clarendon
(received August 1)

(Extract)   *Therapia, July* 23, 1855

Omer Pasha is still here. He has been most graciously received, and also most generously rewarded by the Sultan, who has conferred a considerable grant of land upon him. I need not add that he is on excellent terms with His Majesty's Ministers, and particularly with the Seraskier Pasha. His Highness, accompanied by the last-mentioned Minister, called upon me yesterday. He is expected to leave on his return to the Crimea in four or five days.

With respect to the dangers which threaten Turkey from the side of Kars, he proposes to add 25,000 men to the 10,000 or 12,000 at Batoom; to place himself at their head, and to make an incursion towards Georgia, starting from Redoute-Kaleh, and turning Kutais to good account.

This idea was debated last night in a Council at the Grand Vizier's, and the result of the deliberations, as communicated to the Embassy through M. Pisani, was, that the troops to be employed in the above-mentioned manner under the command of Omer, should be taken from Eupatoria to the amount of

20,000, and from Bulgaria to the amount of 5,000, and that the Contingent, with its numbers completed, should occupy the vacant space at Eupatoria. By way of alternative, it is proposed that if the above-mentioned plan be deemed objectionable, it might be so far modified as to take only 10,000 men from the Crimea, and 15,000 from Bulgaria, including those destined to form part of the Contingent.

The Council professes itself ready to listen to any other suggestion proceeding from the two Embassies, in case that neither one nor the other of the preceding plans should be accepted.

I must confine myself, from want of time, to a statement of these leading points. My personal impression is that Eupatoria would be an advantageous position for the more complete organisation of the Contingent; that the absence of Omer Pasha from before Sebastopol, supposing the troops to remain there under a suitable commander, would be free from the objections lying against any serious diminution of their numbers, and that it might even be productive of some beneficial results.

I propose to communicate on the whole subject freely with my French colleague, and, after advising the Porte to the best of our judgment, to refer to the Commanders-in-chief, and to report again to your Lordship. It is, of course to be understood that my course of opinion is guided by a knowledge of your Lordship's objection to a premature employment of General Vivian's corps.

Brigadier-General Williams to the Earl of Clarendon
(received August 24)

My Lord,   *Kars, July* 28, 1855

The enemy still occupies the camps indicated in my despatch of the 21st instant; but having learned from spies that General Mouravieff intended to move the bulk of his army from Boyouk-Tikmeh to Komansoor, a village only an hour's march to the south-east of our camp entrenchments, every effort has been made to strengthen them, and by four days' cheerful but incessant labour, the Infantry has completed five rows of *trous de loups* round the redoubts and breastworks, extending 6,000 yards; these conical holes, three feet in diameter and three feet deep, add much to our power of resistance.

The enemy's powerful Cavalry still block up the roads leading to Erzeroom and Ardahan, and destroy the growing crops; his Transport Department, as I have already informed your Lordship, is enormous; yesterday a convoy of 5,000 waggons passed towards their great camp, protected by every possible combination on the part of the enemy.

I beg to bring under your Lordship's notice the state of the clothing of this army, and to suggest that immediate steps be taken by the authorities at Constantinople to prepare and forward, without delay, the winter supply, including fezes, cloaks, shoes, and boots; and I also trust that money may be sent to Erzeroom, with orders to Tahir Pasha to cause large supplies of biscuit to be baked, and, above all, a land-carriage (consisting of camels and arabas) to be organised, this army being totally deficient of such an indispensable necessity.

W. F. WILLIAMS

Lord Stratford de Redcliffe to the Earl of Clarendon
(received August 8)

(Extract) *Therapia, July* 30, 1855

The unfavourable judgment passed by Her Majesty's Government on the plans which have been lately under discussion, with a view to the relief of the Sultan's army at Kars, has naturally increased the Porte's embarrassment. It was my duty to make it known to the Turkish Ministers, not only as an opinion, but, with respect to General Vivian's Contingent, as a veto. A most serious dilemma is the immediate result. Her Majesty's Government not only withhold the Contingent, but express a decided preference for the alternative of sending reinforcements to Erzeroom by the way of Trebizond. This opinion is not adopted by the Porte, or indeed by any official or personal authority here. The Seraskier, Omer Pasha, General Guyon, and our own officers, as far as I have means of knowing, agree with the Porte and the French Embassy in preferring a diversion on the side of Redoute-Kaleh, as offering better chances of success, supposing, of course, that the necessary means of transport supply and other indispensable wants can be sufficiently provided. France is at the same time decidedly adverse to any diminution of force in the Crimea; and Omer Pasha, ready to place himself at the head of an Asiatic expedition, requires for that purpose a part of the troops now there.

Such being the present state of the case, I am precluded from contributing to the Porte's extrication from its difficulties, otherwise than by countenancing some new location of the Contingent, which, without exposing the corps to a premature trial, might enable a force of the same amount to be detached for service elsewhere.

No final decision has yet been taken by the Porte. My colleague the French Ambassador has written for General Pélissier's opinion, and Omer Pasha is still in attendance on his Government.

Meanwhile the advices from Kars are not encouraging, and time of precious value is unavoidably wasted in doubt and uncertainty.

AUGUST 1855

The Earl of Clarendon to Lord Cowley

My Lord,   *Foreign Office, August* 1, 1855

I transmit to your Excellency herewith a copy of a despatch [Lord Stratford de Redcliffe to the Earl of Clarendon, dated July 23, 1855] from Viscount Stratford de Redcliffe, respecting the suggestions made by Omer Pasha during his visit to Constantinople, for the relief of the Turkish army at Kars; and with reference to that passage in which his Excellency states that the result of the deliberations of the Divan was, that the troops to be employed in the manner suggested by Omer Pasha, and under his command, should be taken from Eupatoria to the amount of 20,000 men, and from Bulgaria to the amount of 5,000, and that the British Contingent, with its numbers completed, should occupy the vacant space at Eupatoria. I have to state to your Excellency that Her Majesty's Government are favourably disposed to this proposition, and they hope that the Government of the Emperor will concur in it.

CLARENDON

Lord Cowley to the Earl of Clarendon
(Telegraphic)   *Paris, August* 2, 1855, 2.15 P.M.
Count Walewski foresees objections to the proposal contained in your despatch of yesterday.

He will submit it, however, to the Emperor, and hopes to give me His Majesty's answer on Saturday.

Lord Stratford de Redcliffe to the Earl of Clarendon
(received August 16)
My Lord,   *Therapia, August* 2, 1855
The closing words of your Lordship's despatch of the 19th ultimo are, I apprehend, but too likely to be realised. Whatever supplies have been forwarded to the army at Kars since it became known at Constantinople that the Russians had advanced on that side may reach Erzeroom, but have only a slender chance of going beyond. I would observe at the

same time that, little as the Turkish authorities have done themselves credit by their treatment of the army, they hardly deserve the imputation which is conveyed by the preceding words of your Lordship's despatch. Tardy and incomplete as their measures were, notwithstanding the frequent remonstrances and earnest recommendations of Her Majesty's Embassy, attention, to a certain degree, had been paid to the wants of the army, and my correspondence bears witness to much that was done, even under the perverse administration of Riza Pasha, towards the supply of those wants. It is a mistake to attribute the deficiency to a wilful neglect of the Asiatic troops. The troops in Europe were naturally the first object of the Porte's solicitude, and those troops enjoyed the advantage of being commanded by Omer Pasha. But they also experienced, in a less degree, the effects of a bad administrative system, not less corrupt in the military than other departments, and above all of inadequate finances and an exhausted Treasury. I never can forget that when a portion of Omer Pasha's army entered Bucharest on the retreat of the Russians, a regiment of the Sultan's Guards was described by Mr Colquhoun as marching with bare feet over roads covered with snow.

STRATFORD DE REDCLIFFE

The Earl of Clarendon to Lord Cowley
(Extract)   *Foreign Office, August* 3, 1855
Her Majesty's Government have learnt with regret by your Excellency's telegraphic despatch of yesterday

that Count Walewski does not concur with them in the opinion that Omer Pasha and a portion of the army under his command might be sent to Asia to effect a diversion for the relief of Kars and the adjoining country, now menaced by the Russian forces under General Mouravieff, while their place in the Crimea might be filled up by the Turco-British Contingent under Lieutenant-General Vivian.

Her Majesty's Government, however, consider the relief of the Turkish troops in Asia of such vital importance, that they cannot abstain from laying before the Government of the Emperor the various arguments by which they consider the plan recommended by them may be supported.

It is plain that without assistance the whole Turkish force in Asia must be destroyed or captured. The force at Kars is surrounded, and even if able to defend its position against assault, which may be doubted, it must surrender when its provisions are exhausted, and that will happen in a few weeks. The immediate result would be that 13,000 Turkish troops would become prisoners of war, and a strong position be occupied by the Russians.

But, moreover, Kars taken, Erzeroom must share the like fate, and the whole of the neighbouring country would be in the hands of the Russians, while the season would be too far advanced for military operations to drive them out of it.

If, on the other hand, the allies do not take Sebastopol before the winter, the Russians, by occupying Asia Minor, will have a considerable advantage over the allies, and as the Russians have nothing to do on the Danube, and are free from apprehension anywhere to the north of the Danube, they can send into Georgia, and thence into Asia Minor, a force of considerable magnitude. This would be striking a serious blow to the Turkish Empire, and one the effects of which it would be difficult to remedy. If, on the other hand, Omer Pasha were to go to Redoute-Kaleh or Erzeroom with a sufficient force, the Russians would be driven back, or forced to retire.

Omer Pasha's knowledge of Asiatic Turkey would give him advantages in carrying on war there which no other Commander can possess, while in the Crimea his presence is comparatively of no value.

Her Majesty's Government indeed feel doubtful whether, if the Turkish Government should desire to avail itself of Omer Pasha's special qualification for service in Asia, any just objections could be made to the Porte's utilising in that quarter the services of one who has proved himself to be so able a Commander, and who has succeeded in organising an efficient army at a moment when some of the most important provinces of the Turkish Empire are invaded by the enemy, and where a considerable Turkish force is in danger of being made prisoners of war.

Her Majesty's Government would doubt whether it was wise, even if they felt sure that they had the right to do so, to object to the adoption by the Porte of such a course, especially as the transfer of the Contingent under Lieutenant-General Vivian either to Balaklava or to Eupatoria, whichever might be deemed best, would fill up, or nearly so, the void occasioned by the removal of Omer Pasha and a portion of his force to Asia Minor, and the reinforcements sent to Lieutenant-General Vivian and to the British and French armies would add still further to the aggregate force of the allied armies in the Crimea.

Her Majesty's Government wish that your Excellency should submit these observations without delay to the French Government, in the hope that they may be induced to take a different view of the question from that which they have hitherto entertained, and may enable your Excellency to convey to Viscount Stratford de Redcliffe by the messenger of tomorrow, while a similar communication is made to M. de Thouvenel by the French Government, authority to recommend the Porte to adopt the course of detaching Omer Pasha and an adequate portion of his army to Asia Minor, so that by this means the only resource which now remains for averting from the Turkish army in Asia the great disaster which there is too much reason to apprehend is impending over it, may at all events not be left untried.

Brigadier-General Williams to the Earl of Clarendon
(received August 29)

My Lord,   *Kars, August* 3, 1855
On the 31st ultimo General Mouravieff broke up his camp at Boyouk-Tikmeh, and stationed 15 battalions of Infantry, 1 regiment of Dragoons, 2 regiments of Cossacks, 500 Irregular Cavalry, and 40 guns, in a

defensible position at Komansoor, about one hour to the south of us. With the remaining half of his army, the Russian General again moved towards the mountain-pass of Soghanli-Dagh, on the Erzeroom road. I observed his camp-fires yesterday at daybreak, from the heights above Kars, distant eight hours from us, but none were visible this morning.

Veli Pasha has been informed of this movement on the part of the enemy, and I have also written to Major Olpherts on the subject. If we are to credit the reports brought in by our spies, General Mouravieff meditates an advance upon Erzeroom, but I believe his object to be the devastation of the country, and more especially the destruction of the growing crops, in which barbarous measures the army now in our front is daily occupied.

We steadily add to the strength of our field-works, and yesterday we seized the cattle of the surrounding villages, to prevent their falling into the hands of the enemy, and to add to the chance of our holding out till relieved by the allies.

We are enabled to procure small sums of money from merchants, by giving favourable exchanges for sovereigns on the Erzeroom Military Defterdar, but I regret to state that he has so far forgotten his duty, as to refuse the payment of those bills, for which, I trust, he will be called to account by the Seraskier. It is thus that the Turks will upset every combination and chance of success for a few piastres of agio, whilst they themselves hesitate not to rob by wholesale.

The most active civil functionary in this camp is Kiarami Effendi, who is worthy of any reward which the Mushir may apply for, and I beg to recommend him to the good offices of your Lordship.

The spirits and disposition of the troops are excellent. We have still nearly two months' provision, except barley, which has failed us, our carriage communications with Erzeroom being entirely cut off.

W. F. WILLIAMS

Lord Cowley to the Earl of Clarendon
(Telegraphic) *Paris, August* 4, 1855, 3.15 P.M.
The French Government will not oppose the projected expedition to Asia Minor, under Omer Pasha, provided that the numbers of the Turkish Contingent before Sebastopol are not diminished.

The Earl of Clarendon to Lord Stratford de Redcliffe
(Extract) *Foreign Office, August* 4, 1855
My despatch to Lord Cowley of yesterday's date contains a full statement of the grounds on which Her Majesty's Government consider such a movement under Omer Pasha advisable, and I have received this afternoon from his Excellency the telegraphic message which I enclose [see above], announcing that the French Government will not oppose the desired expedition.

Immediately on receipt of this message, I sent to your Excellency a despatch in the following terms:

August 4. Omer Pasha can go to relieve Kars, provided he does not diminish the Turkish troops before Sebastopol, or disturb the garrison of Yenikale.

Desire Vivian to hold himself in readiness to go to Eupatoria with his Turkish Contingent.

Consul Brant to the Earl of Clarendon
(received August 29)

My Lord,   *Erzeroom, August* 7, 1855
I have the honour to enclose the copies of four despatches I addressed to his Excellency the Viscount Stratford de Redcliffe. I might have condensed them, but I preferred giving things in detail, that your Lordship might the better judge of the total incompetency of the Turkish officers to command military operations.

General Williams is now beleaguered in Kars, and must be starved out, if succours are not sent. The country around Kars has no resources left, and they have nothing to hope for but from strong reinforcements. It is, I confess, beyond my comprehension, how the Russians have been allowed, without control, to ravage the country; it will bring on a famine I expect, or else unheard-of dearness of food, and it would be difficult to estimate the immense loss of property which has been already incurred, and the still greater which may be anticipated.

JAS. BRANT

Enclosure 1

Consul Brant to Lord Stratford de Redcliffe

My Lord,   *Erzeroom, August* 3, 1855

I have the honour to report to your Excellency that yesterday, late in the evening, a report was spread that the Russians had reached Kupri-Keuy, and that the force under Veli Pasha was in full retreat on Erzeroom. I did not give credit to this rumour, as we hear so many similar every day; but near 11 o'clock at night, Hafiz Pasha called at my house, and when I heard of his being at the door, I went down: he was on horseback, and accompanied by a guard; he took me aside and told me that credible information had come that the Russians were actually at Kupri-Keuy, but he did not appear to know with certainty that Veli Pasha had retreated before them.

At past midnight the Defterdar sent me a letter informing me that Veli Pasha's force was on its retreat towards Erzeroom, and inviting me to attend a Council to be held next morning. I went, hoping to ascertain the real state of matters; but I found none of the Military Pashas there, but only the members of the Civil Medjlis, the Musteshar, the two Defterdars, Civil and Military, the Armenian Bishop, and some of the chiefs of the trading community. The Austrian Consul was already there, and the French soon joined the Assembly. No individual took the lead; no one seemed to know the object of the meeting; and a great deal of desultory conversation took place, which tended to no result, except the issue of an order that no families should quit the city, to prevent alarm spreading, and likewise an order to send some Bashi-Bozouks to occupy a by-pass, leading from the Plain of Passin into that of Erzeroom, which had not been fortified or noticed. I remarked that this was not a Military Council, and that such questions belonged to the General commanding, and should be proposed to the Council of War. It did not seem to be clear who was the commanding officer, and nobody knew exactly whither all the Military Pashas had gone to, nor on what errand.

On leaving me last night Hafiz Pasha went up to the forts and arranged for manning the guns, and mounting others, as well as placing Bashi-Bozouks in the redoubts. This morning several large guns were mounted in the forts. I left the Council without having learned anything to be depended on with regard to the Russians; but the French Consul, who had been at a village on the Plain of Passin, the day before, hearing of the Russian force being at Kupri-Keuy, came into town, and found the roads so choked with flying men, women, and children, mixed up with Bashi-Bozouks, as to render them almost impassable. All the villages were abandoned, the cattle left at the mercy of the Koords, who were driving them off, and then burning the houses. The evil of this will be very serious, even if it goes no further, the loss immense, and the replacing of so much food very difficult; and it is the more to be regretted, as very little foresight and attention to the army of Asia might have obviated the misery, the desolation, and the loss of property which must ensue.

The Division of Veli Pasha, increased by the garrison here, and reinforcements, though small, which have been gradually joining, should render the Turkish force, well commanded and occupying a strong position, as it now does, on the Pass of the Dévéboyonou, one hour and a half from the city, quite capable of making a successful resistance to the Russian invading force, which is variously represented at from 12,000 to 17,000 men of all arms, the most, I should say, Irregulars. There are hordes of Bashi-Bozouks here, who behave as usual— cowardly towards the enemy, cruelly towards their friends, and who, useless as they are, eat up the country, and cost what would support a small, useful, regular force, which might do real service in the field, and that the Bashi-Bozouks never did and never will do.

JAS. BRANT

Enclosure 2

Consul Brant to Lord Stratford de Redcliffe

My Lord,   *Erzeroom, August* 4, 1855

I have the honour to report to your Excellency, that today all the Pashas have been out at the camp at the Dévéboyonou.

There were innumerable reports as to the movements of the Russians, but it appears that they have not advanced, but are encamped at the village of Hassan-Kaleh, at a distance of about three leagues

[4 miles] from the entrenched position of the Turkish force on the Dévéboyonou.

In the evening at about 6 o'clock, Hafiz Pasha came into town; and having made my preparations and hired horses, I addressed him a note, requesting an escort for my family, which I thought it prudent to remove under the circumstances.

He expressed regret that I had come to such a determination, as it would spread alarm in the city, but he promised to call the next day and arrange the matter.

Another object I had in view was to learn some particulars of the relative forces of the Russians and Turks, and the probable result of the advance of the former; but his room was so crowded with persons, that my dragoman could not speak a word to him privately, but he only learned generally that the Russian force was estimated at between 800 to 1,200 men, with twelve or sixteen guns, while Hafiz Pasha reckoned the whole Turkish force at the entrenched position, in the redoubts around the town, and in the city, at about 20,000 or 25,000, if not 30,000 men of all arms, but mostly Bashi-Bozouks.

My dragoman also heard that Hafiz Pasha was of opinion that the Russians should be attacked, as he considered it disgraceful to allow them the complete possession of the plain with an inferior force, and that in consequence of his difference of opinion from the other Pashas, he had retired from the camp. He inferred from the Pasha's expressions that he was disgusted with the Commanders of the army.

I received this morning a note from Major Olpherts, from the Turkish camp. He said their positions could not be forced in front, and could not be taken unless by surprise, or by being outflanked. He thought the Russian force could not exceed 8,000 men, with ten or fourteen guns, as reported; and unless it was reinforced from Kars, there was no danger.

The Major does not allude to there being confusion or disorder in the camp, though I heard that it existed.

JAS. BRANT

Enclosure 3

Consul Brant to Lord Stratford de Redcliffe
(Extract)   *Erzeroom, August* 6, 1855
I have the honour to inform your Excellency, that yesterday several of the Pashas came from the camp to attend a Council, which was attended by a great many of the principal Turks.

After its breaking up, Hafiz Pasha called on me on his way to the camp. He would scarcely wait to allow me time to ask a question. He wished me to defer the departure of my family, in order not to alarm the public; but as I pressed for a guard, remarking that women and children could but add to the confusion, he promised one should be ready for this morning. I told him that I had myself no intention to depart until the last moment.

He complained that his Bashi-Bozouks were unprovided with tents, and exposed to the heat of the sun by day, and the cold air by night, and were falling sick and deserting. They were allowed but a small loaf of bad bread. Their conduct inspires a great alarm in the town, and all the shops are closed. The Pasha said he must go to the camp to speak a word of encouragement to his men, or they would all desert.

The French Consul yesterday morning received advices from the camp, which not being explicit or encouraging, he proposed riding out to ascertain the real state of matters. Towards evening he returned: the Russian camp was in the same position it was at first, and the troops had not made any movement.

At the camp everything was in the greatest state of confusion; guns, shot, and ammunition in distant places; no preparations made for a defence; no knowledge of the extent of the enemy's force; and no one seemed employed to any useful purpose. In short, it appeared to the Consul, that were the Russians to have made an attack, scarce any attempt at resistance would have been made. He estimated the Turkish force at from 8,000 to 10,000—about 6,000 Infantry, Cavalry, and Artillery, and the rest Bashi-Bozouks. This, I think, from all I can learn, is about correct. There are nearly 40 good guns.

Veli Pasha commands the regular troops; Mehmed Pasha, our Vali, all the Bashi-Bozouks, except the Trebizond and Lazistan, which are under Hafiz Pasha.

There seems to be great jealousy and want of cordial understanding amongst the Commanders, none of whom seem to possess the requisite qualities of judgment, military knowledge, and courage.

The Bashi-Bozouks go out to camp and come in when they think proper, and are apparently under no sort of control.

In the evening Hafiz Pasha came into town, and sent me a message to beg I would not quit in the morning, as the Russians had retreated, and we should confer together on the subject on the morrow. It had been observed that the Russians had moved their tents in the afternoon, but as it is their custom, this was not supposed to indicate any movement of consequence; but the Mudir of Hassan-Kaleh sent word to the camp that the Russians had gone to Kupri-Keuy. The motive of this retreat is unknown as yet.

Enclosure 4

Consul Brant to Lord Stratford de Redcliffe

My Lord,   *Erzeroom, August* 7, 1855

I have the honour to report to your Excellency that the Russians have retreated on the Kars road, having razed the earthworks at Kupri-Keuy, for which purpose they took with them 200 Armenians from Hassan-Kaleh; and they further took 100 araba-loads of grain from Government stores.

Everything that I have stated in my three last despatches has been fully confirmed by trustworthy persons, but I have not spoken with sufficient severity of the imbecile and cowardly conduct of the Pashas; they would undoubtedly have run away if they had been attacked, although, with the number of guns they had, their position, if tolerably well defended, could not have been forced by an enemy treble the numbers of the Russians. It is pretty certain they had not above 8,000 men in all, with 10 guns. The conduct as well of the Pashas as of the Laz, destroys all confidence in the safety of the town; if attacked, it will probably, in such case, be plundered both by the defenders and the enemy; and I have thought it prudent to remove my family to Trebizond.

JAS. BRANT

Brigadier-General Williams to the Earl of Clarendon
(received September 19)

My Lord,   *Kars, August* 10, 1855

I had the honour, on the 3rd instant, of acquainting your Lordship with the movement of General Mouravieff towards Erzeroom, and I have since learned that prior to that advance, the Russian General had received a reinforcement of a regiment of Infantry from Georgia, making up a total of 33 battalions of Infantry. The force he left to observe us consisted of 18 battalions of Infantry, three regiments of Cavalry, and 54 guns. As neither our numbers (which I abstain from stating) nor our organisation could hold out a chance of success in any attack upon such an army as now observes us, I have advised the Mushir still further to strengthen his entrenchments, and this counsel his Excellency has steadily carried out, through the zealous superintendence of Colonel Lake.

During the absence of the Russian Commander-in-chief, the General in command of the corps of observation has kept our garrison on the alert, more especially his Cavalry, which, from its superior numbers and discipline, is master of the neighbourhood. But on the 8th instant, the enemy, losing sight of his usual precautions, advanced with large masses of Infantry, Cavalry, and Artillery, to within gun-shot of the Kanly Tabia, on the south-east angle of our entrenched camp, when a well-directed fire from the guns of that redoubt obliged him to retire with the loss of several officers and many men.

With regard to the movements of General Mouravieff, I learn through a verbal message from Veli Pasha, sent by an orderly dragoon from the close vicinity of the Dévéboyonou, that he had executed his instructions by falling back from Kupri-Keuy on that Pass, which I had selected, and in part fortified, before I left Erzeroom; but I am still ignorant of what has subsequently taken place between the two armies in that neighbourhood, although a week has elapsed since the arrival of the orderly dragoon above alluded to. If, however, we can believe a man who has just reached Kars from the Soghanli-Dagh, and who assures me that General Mouravieff's corps d'armée was camped last night on this side of that mountain-pass, and consequently in the Plain of Kars, I must draw the gratifying conclusion, that he has found Veli Pasha's position, joined to the fortifications of Erzeroom, too strong to molest without losses which he was not prepared to risk.

Be this as it may, I trust the allies will, by a prompt diversion in Georgia, oblige General Mouravieff to retire; otherwise nothing can save Kars from falling into his hands. We are now on two-thirds of our ration of bread, and the cattle seized from the villages will not supply animal food for anything like the period named in my last despatch. The horses of the Cavalry and Artillery begin to feel the want of barley, and will soon be unfit for service.

W. F. WILLIAMS

Lord Stratford de Redcliffe to the Earl of Clarendon
(received August 24)

My Lord,   *Therapia, August* 12, 1855

From the conversation which I held this morning with Omer Pasha, and also from what passed at my interview, as mentioned elsewhere, with the Ottoman Secretary of State, I conclude that the Porte is firmly resolved on attempting to relieve the army at Kars, by a diversion from some point of the coast near, if not exactly at, Redoute-Kaleh.

Your Lordship is already apprised of the grounds on which opinions are entertained in favour of that plan. The Ottoman Commander-in-chief is fully convinced that any attempt to operate by the way of Trebizond and Erzeroom would prove abortive. Besides the want of time and difficulties occasioned by the badness of the road, his Highness argues that on no military calculation could he reckon upon being able to meet on equal terms the Russian army now engaged in besieging Kars, and advancing on Erzeroom.

The Porte is to hold a Council this afternoon, and Omer Pasha is to be present at its deliberations. The decision, whatever it may be, at its close, will be communicated to the two Embassies, and the principle of abstaining from any mode of action calculated to impede or discourage the general operations of the alliance appeared to meet with the full admission [consent] of Fuad Pasha.

STRATFORD DE REDCLIFFE

Consul Brant to the Earl of Clarendon
(received September 3)

My Lord,   *Erzeroom, August* 13, 1855
I have the honour to enclose a copy of a despatch I this day addressed to Her Majesty's Ambassador at the Porte.

It is painful for me to repeat so often the same disgusting tale of incompetency in the Governors and Chiefs, of venality, corruption, and cowardice in all classes; but I conceive I should not be doing my duty were I to shrink from exposing these things, in order that your Lordship may form a true estimate of the difficulties to be encountered in remedying these crying evils.

There should be here a General like General Williams, with sufficient authority to keep the Turkish Pashas to their duty, otherwise they will never do it, in defending their country. Although there are troops here wasting their time in perfect idleness, yet bands of Koords are allowed to complete the ruin of the poor inhabitants of the Plain of Passin, which the Russians only partially effected.

Our Vali, Mehmed Pasha, is in the camp with a number of irregular soldiers, and witnessing the terrified inhabitants flying from the Koords who had driven them from their homes, does nothing to protect them, nor to avert the dreadful calamities inflicted on them by their fellow subjects.

I have often represented how useless these Koords were as subjects to the Sultan, and how dangerous in time of war with Russia, yet but very partial and ineffectual attempts have been made to keep them under control; and now they are entirely freed from it, they prove themselves worse foes to their Sovereign than the armies of a nation with whom he is at open war.

JAS. BRANT

Enclosure

Consul Brant to Lord Stratford de Redcliffe
(Extract)   *Erzeroom, August* 13, 1855

I have the honour to report to your Excellency that the Russian force which invaded Hassan-Kaleh, after retiring, divided itself, one portion taking the road to Kars, the other retracing its steps to Toprak-Kaleh. The Turkish army retains its position at the Dévéboyonou, waiting, it is said, orders from the Mushir at Kars, although there has been a talk of its resuming its position at Kupri-Keuy, leaving the defences of the Dévéboyonou to the Bashi-Bozouk. Every day, nay every hour, shows that the military officers of rank are worse than incompetent. There is no union amongst them; each asserting his right to command, and intriguing against the others, to the detriment of discipline and efficiency, and to the ruin of the Sultan's cause; and yet the resources for defence are immense—sufficient, if well employed, to resist General Mouravieff's whole army; but the capacity is wanting: every officer is trying to appropriate to himself power for the sake of securing a good share of plunder, and instead of considering how he can best serve his country, thinks only of serving his own selfish purposes.

The Bashi-Bozouks commit, as usual, every kind of excess, and desert in crowds; they are the terror of the inhabitants, and more dreaded than the Russians. Provisions are getting scarce, and increasing in price; disease is spreading amongst an ill-fed, ill-sheltered, and reckless crowd of lawless men, who are brought hither by compulsion, and have neither the courage nor the inclination to fight in the cause of the Sultan, and who destroy the resources of the country as they pass and repass through it. There must have arrived up to this time near 30,000, and I should estimate that the force remaining can scarce amount to 10,000; it is said that a further number of 15,000 will soon arrive.

Reports are continually spread of attacks on Kars, successfully repulsed, countenanced by, if not originating with, the military authorities; so that one doubts everything one hears. This is a system with the Turks, but what it can tend to but distrust and discouragement, it would be difficult to imagine.

When I ascertained that the retreat of the Russians was a reality and not a feint, I deferred the removal of my family to avoid the great expense, inconvenience, and danger.

Brigadier-General Williams to the Earl of Clarendon
(received September 10)

(Extract)   *Kars, August* 15, 1855

By the last messenger I had the honour to inform your Lordship of the report brought in as to the return of General Mouravieff to the plain of Kars; I am now enabled to confirm this intelligence, and to state that the united Russian army is encamped in front of the key to our entrenched position, to the defences of which we have added and still continue to add.

A messenger yesterday reached us from Veli Pasha from the fortified position of the Pass of Dévéboyonou near Erzeroom, from which it appears that General Mouravieff retired without attempting to force it; and I have reason to believe that Hafiz Pasha made, in the meantime, every effort to put the new forts around Erzeroom in a proper state of defence.

The demonstration which the enemy recently made against Kanly Tabia, of which I had the honour to acquaint your Lordship by the last messenger, cost them a general officer, a Colonel, five Captains, and 220 sub-officers and men. We witnessed from the heights the funeral of an officer of high rank, and the preparations for burying their dead. The fire of our Artillery was most creditable, obliging that of the enemy to retire after firing four rounds.

General Mouravieff's army now before us, consists of 28 battalions of Infantry, 6,000 Cavalry, and 76 guns; 5 battalions, with Irregular Horse and 4 guns, must be added to this force—they are employed in escorting the convoys from Gumri.

The enemy's Cavalry is now so stationed on the Erzeroom roads as to cut off every source of information or supply.

P.S. A peasant, well acquainted with the country, will endeavour to take this despatch over the mountains.

The Earl of Clarendon to Lord Stratford de Redcliffe
My Lord,   *Foreign Office, August* 16, 1855
With reference to your Excellency's despatch of the 2nd instant, respecting supplies to the army of Kars, I have to inform you that Her Majesty's Government have much reason to doubt whether the supplies which Riza Pasha informed you he had forwarded to the army at Kars ever reached their destination, or ever left Constantinople.

CLARENDON

Lieutenant-Colonel Simmons to the Earl of Clarendon
(received August 29)
My Lord,   *Constantinople, August* 20, 1855
I have to inform your Lordship that an aide-de-camp of the Seraskier arrived last evening from Kars, which

he left about fifteen days since, having taken his departure by night, and carefully avoiding in his route the most frequented roads. He was not the bearer of despatches, as it appeared dangerous to entrust him with written documents, for fear of his falling into the enemy's hands.

He reports that, at the time of his departure, the stores within the town of Kars did not contain more than sufficient provisions for the garrison for one month, or five weeks at the outside, and that they were not well provided with ammunition. This, however, does not appear to be of much consequence, as General Mouravieff had proclaimed to his army, which, by the reinforcements it has received, is stated now to number about 50,000 men, to reduce the town of Kars by starvation, and to capture the garrison without firing a shot.

It is evident that his proceedings correspond with this announcement, for the Russians have not opened trenches against the town, and merely content themselves with a strict blockade.

They have caused the inhabitants to remove everything in the shape of provisions throughout a district within a radius of eight hours (28 miles) round Kars as a centre.

The Russians had advanced, and shown themselves within ten miles of Erzeroom, the Turks not being in sufficient force to oppose them at Kupri-Keuy, about 30 miles from Erzeroom, where they had thrown up some entrenchments to cover the town. The Russians, however, had since fallen back again towards Kars.

The force at Erzeroom consists of 6,000 Regular troops, and 12,000 Irregular, but many of these latter are leaving and dispersing.

I learned the above from Omer Pasha this morning, and from his conversation it is evident that the Porte are deeply impressed with the deplorable state of affairs in Asia, and are almost in despair at the apparent certainty of losing, towards the end of this month or early in September, the garrison of Kars, 16,000 men, with nearly 200 pieces of artillery, of which about 70 are field guns.

It would appear, from the Pasha's observations, that they attribute this approaching disaster primarily to the mismanagement and neglect of affairs by the late Government, and look upon Reshid and Riza Pashas as especially culpable.

It would appear also that they are very much grieved and disappointed at the time which has been lost in endeavouring to recover their position, and save the garrison of Kars, and that the Cabinets of Paris and London, as well as the military authorities in the Crimea, have not considered the subject in that serious aspect in which it presents itself to the Porte, but have objected to the propositions which have hitherto been made with a view to retrieving their position and preventing the disaster.

Omer Pasha has authorised me to state as his opinion, that he feels satisfied that the effect will be very shortly felt, probably within a few weeks, by the advance of the enemy's cavalry, which is very numerous, and by a prohibition which he will impose upon the inhabitants to prevent all articles of provision from being brought to Trebizond, Samsoon, and Sinope, for exportation for the use of the allies.

Some of the Koords, it appears, have already joined the Russians, and probably a decisive success at Kars will take effect on the Persians.

The result will be that a great part of the Asiatic dominions of the Porte, with its resources in men, money, and provisions, will be lost for a time at least to the Turks.

The loss of revenue will be most seriously felt by the Turks in the prosecution of the war; and Omer Pasha appears to think that there may even be difficulty in keeping the soldiers of the army of Roumelia together, as they have been in great measure recruited in Asia, and hearing that their country is open to the Russians, without any force, however small, to oppose their progress through it, they will naturally, if not sent, seek to desert, with the hope of saving their families from the hands of the enemy.

The whole of these considerations, which press with great weight on the Porte, cause Omer Pasha more than ever to desire to make a decided movement with the least possible loss of time, with the troops, according to the proposition which I forwarded to your Lordship in my despatch of the 16th instant.

For this reason he hopes to obtain the assistance of France and England for the conveyance of his troops and for provisioning his army; for he says that without it the Turks alone cannot perform the operation within a reasonable time, and therefore the small force, 6,000 men, in Erzeroom, will be dispersed, making, with the garrison of Kars, a loss of 22,000 men to the common cause, besides a numerous artillery.

From the turn affairs have taken, he appears to consider it questionable where the point of disembarkation should be, but must leave its determination to the development of events and to the movements which the Russians may hereafter decide on making.

J. L. A. SIMMONS

Brigadier-General Williams to the Earl of Clarendon
(received September 19)

(Extract)   *Kars, August* 21, 1855

Since I had the honour to address your Lordship on the 15th instant, the enemy's Infantry and Artillery have remained in the camp they then occupied. The Cavalry, supported by Horse Artillery and rockets, however, has taken a strong hill-position to the northwest, about an hour's march from our lines, and assisted by his numerous Irregular Horse, cuts off all communications with Erzeroom, *via* Olti, with Ardahan, or indeed any other place from whence we could draw supplies of any kind.

A convoy of 3,000 arabas, or country carts, and 2,000 camels, is now in sight coming from Gumri. Battering guns, drawn by bullocks, accompany this convoy. I have, therefore, requested Colonel Lake to convert the barbette battery of Kanly Tabia into one with embrasures, and to take such measures for strengthening the armament of this and other works as the occasion requires.

The weather is oppressively hot, yet the troops are in excellent health; the hospital list amounting to 289.

Should Her Majesty's Government and its allies determine on making Trebizond the base of future operations against Georgia, I still trust that an immediate and powerful demonstration will be made by a Turkish army from Redoute-Kaleh; and for the present defence of Erzeroom, I would beg strongly to urge the landing of a division of General Vivian's force at Trebizond, and a rapid advance upon Erzeroom, so as to ensure the retention of that important fortified post in the hands of the allies, even if this division of the Contingent found itself unable to succour us.

Brigadier-General Williams to the Earl of Clarendon
(received October 1)

My Lord,   *Kars, August* 25, 1855

The Russian Cavalry, which now amounts to 8,000, has so narrowed the circle from which we cut our forage and scanty supply of barley in the ear, that detailed orders will be forwarded by this courier to Tahir Pasha, the Chief of the Military Medjlis of Erzeroom, and also to Mehmed Pasha, the Governor-General of the Province, to endeavour to throw convoys (however small) of barley into Kars. Directions will also accompany these orders with regard to the storing of the harvest now reaping in and around the city of Erzeroom.

I am sorry to inform your Lordship that great apathy reigns at Erzeroom from the highest functionary to the lowest; every Pasha and Bey who has been charged with missions from this camp to that city has, in his turn, disappeared from the scene—a scene from which all of high rank are glad to escape. I therefore trust that, through your Lordship's representations, they may receive from the Porte the most stringent orders to execute the directions forwarded to them by the Mushir.

We have just heard that one of the detachments of Infantry and Cavalry (under Coblian Ali Bey) which so harass us, has marched towards Ahkiska, which place is menaced by an incursion of Irregulars, by order of Mustafa Pasha of Batoom. This will convince your Lordship that a serious demonstration from Redoute-Kaleh would cause the immediate departure of at least a large corps of General Mouravieff's army, whose camps remain where they were when I last had the honour to address your Lordship. A portion of the Irregular Riflemen of Lazistan recently evinced a mutinous spirit, and when caught in the act of pillage by Major Teesdale, drew their weapons upon him. By my insistence the Mushir caused them to be flogged and imprisoned; their rifles and other arms were destroyed in presence of their comrades; and this prompt punishment has completely restored order.

By means of numerous and well-paid spies, the enemy has been able to obtain all the information he desired. I, two days ago, induced the Mushir to try and execute a Mussulman, on whom were found the proofs of his guilt, and the inhabitants of the town expressed great satisfaction at his fate. Another Mussulman is also under sentence, and will be hanged. The Mushir has also proclaimed his determination to shoot all deserters who may again fall into our hands.

In thus taking every precaution against treachery, we cheerfully persevere, in the hope that our long and painful blockade may yet terminate favourably; for the enemy, thus far, does not seem inclined to enter on a more active course towards us.

W. F. Williams

*Lieutenant-Colonel Simmons to the Earl of Clarendon
(received September 5)*

My Lord,   *Constantinople, August* 26, 1855
I have to inform your Lordship that Omer Pasha has stated to me that he will not be able to leave Constantinople for five or six days, as he is occupied in making the necessary arrangements for the expedition to Asia, and his presence here is absolutely required to complete them.

I yesterday was present at a meeting at the Capudan Pasha's, at which the Seraskier and Omer Pasha were present, and when the necessary orders were given for carrying the following arrangements into execution:

According to the calculations then made, the Turkish sailing fleet, consisting of six ships, are capable of carrying, at one time, 5,950 men, or 1,360 horses. The steamers belonging to the Government, seven in number, of which three have been recently purchased, with five others which the Government have either hired or are in the point of hiring, are capable of carrying at one time 10,450 men or 2,060 horses.

Orders were therefore given for these ships, the greater part of which have already proceeded to Sizopolis or Varna, to embark three batteries of Artillery with *matériel* and horses complete, and to fill up entirely with baggage horses, which will proceed at once, the sailing vessels towed by steamers to Batoom.

They will then return and load entirely with Infantry.

Omer Pasha hopes thus to land 15,000 men and 3,420 horses in Asia in two trips of the Turkish fleet alone, the operation occupying from three weeks to a month, or for each voyage from ten days to a fortnight. This calculation, however, may differ very much from the reality, if the weather should prove to be tempestuous, and prevent the sailing ships from being towed.

The baggage horses and artillery being landed, the Pasha hopes that, so soon as the Infantry arrive, he will be able at once to advance with the troops already there, so as to take them out of the unhealthy climate of the coast, and to make some slight demonstration before the arrival of the rest of his troops from the Crimea.

The pontoon train and remainder of the baggage horses will follow according as the means of transport are found.

Omer Pasha is most desirous that assistance should be given by the allies in conveying the troops and their *matériel* from before Sebastopol, and baggage horses from Sizopolis; and he considers the most practicable way in which this could be done, would be by allowing the English fleet to convey the troops on from before Sebastopol to Asia, after having conveyed the Contingent to Balaklava to replace them.

The Pasha intends himself to go to the coast of Asia to examine the positions and obtain information before the first ships can arrive and disembark their freights.

J. L. A. SIMMONS

SEPTEMBER 1855

Brigadier-General Williams to the Earl of Clarendon
(received October 1)

My Lord,   *Kars, September* 1, 1855
Since I addressed your Lordship on the 25th ultimo,
the enemy's Cavalry has received a reinforcement of
2,000 men, and presses, if possible, still more closely on
our picquets and advanced posts, where a daily struggle takes place for forage, which has, for several days,
failed to supply our wants; a large portion, therefore, of

our attenuated Cavalry horses has been sent from the camp, in order to seek subsistence beyond the mountains, and out of the reach of the enemy's Cavalry, which cannot be estimated at less than 10,000. General Mouravieff, with his Infantry and Artillery, occupies the same positions which he held when I last wrote.

It is with the utmost difficulty that either horse or foot messengers escape the vigilance of the enemy, and I abstain from entering into details which might fall into their hands. The garrison preserves its health, notwithstanding the great difference of temperature between day and night; its spirit, I am happy to add, is excellent.

W. F. WILLIAMS

Consul Brant to the Earl of Clarendon
(received October 1)

My Lord,   *Erzeroom, September* 4, 1855
I have the honour to enclose a copy of a despatch I addressed to Viscount Stratford de Redcliffe, yesterday, regarding Kars.

The avowal of Tahir Pasha, that he has not under him a single officer of courage or enterprise, is a lamentable proof, if such were wanting, of the total inefficiency of the Turkish officers. I much fear that General Williams is in a very precarious position, and that the provisions of the garrison will not hold out while succours are coming. Something might have been done before this. The failure in preserving Kars is not merely the defeat of a small force—it is the loss of an immense number of guns, ammunition, and stores of all kinds, which it would take a serious amount of money, and no small exertions, to replace; and besides that, the works made at Kars and here would render both places almost impregnable in the hands of the Russians, and it would demand a summer's campaign, and 50,000 good troops, to recover what 10,000 men, sent up now, might have saved.

I cannot conceive how the Turkish Government can have been so apathetic; it must have been long since informed of the danger of delay, and so small an effort was needed to prevent so terrible a calamity as the loss of Kars and Erzeroom. If Omer Pasha be quick in his movements, he may yet be in time, but delay is fraught with imminent danger; and I shall be very anxious until I hear of the landing of an adequate force at Redoute-Kaleh, as Kars, by that event alone, might, I hope, be saved.

JAS. BRANT

Enclosure

Consul Brant to Lord Stratford de Redcliffe

My Lord,   *Erzeroom, September* 3, 1855

I received a letter from Kars of the 25th August, in which General Williams begged me to urge Tahir Pasha to do something for their relief, observing that a regiment of Cavalry having gone from Kars and passed the Russian posts, it might return, each horseman bringing in two bags of barley. I waited on Tahir

Pasha, and he promised that he would leave nothing undone to relieve the garrison.

At Olti, about half-way, there are stores of everything, but the Commander there, Aali Pasha, is credulous and timid, and is prevented from making attempts to throw in supplies by exaggerated reports he hears of the danger of the undertaking and the certainty of failure. Tahir Pasha observed that Aali Pasha, by his timidity, paralyses those under him who have more energy than himself, and he begged me to represent to General Williams that there is not a single officer amongst all the forces out of Kars who has spirit or enterprise enough to make an attempt at introducing relief, though he were promised promotion for success, as I had suggested.

Tahir Pasha said that he would go himself to Olti and see what he could do, and Major Stuart and Captain Cameron expressed their wish to accompany him, and do their best to assist in an attempt to get into Kars with a body of Cavalry carrying barley.

There are three regiments now outside Kars, reckoning about 1,200 men, beside some Irregular Horse, so that by a successful effort a considerable supply might be introduced, and I should expect that such a body would be too strong to be stopped by any outposts it might encounter, if the trial were made secretly and by the least frequented paths.

General Williams dare not express himself clearly as to his exact position in regard to the stock of provisions, but from what he does say and from what I have heard from other quarters, I much fear that they

are beginning to run very short, and that if such efficient succours as would oblige the Russians to retreat
do not speedily arrive, or supplies cannot be introduced, it will not be possible to hold out until the
snow obliges the enemy to retire.

Omer Pasha was reported to be about to land
immediately at Redoute-Kaleh with 30,000 troops,
but I yesterday heard that he would not embark from
Constantinople before the 1st Muharem, I believe ten
days hence; and when matters begin once to be
deferred, there is no saying how often they may be
again postponed, while every minute's delay may bring
on the catastrophe which is sought to be prevented.

I would therefore represent to your Excellency
the necessity of stimulating the Turkish Government
to hasten forward succours, for if Kars be taken,
Erzeroom must of course fall, and the losses these
events would occasion the Turkish Government are
such as would be beyond its power to repair, and,
besides, an enormous sacrifice of blood and treasure,
a very large army, and a year's campaign, would be
required to recover the two cities, which in the hands
of Russia might become impregnable.

JAS. BRANT

Consul Brant to the Earl of Clarendon
(received October 1)

My Lord,   *Erzeroom, September* 4, 1855
I have the honour to report to your Lordship that a
person who arrived from Kars later than the post,

states that on the 29th August the Russians made a double attack on Kars: one a feint, at the Veli Pasha Tabia, with four battalions, a few guns, and some Bashi-Bozouks; the other, a serious one, with their whole force on the Kanly Tabia.

The first was repulsed by a sortie of some Turkish troops, and the other by the Artillery, which did great execution on the assailants with grape. On their retreat, in confusion, they were followed up by some Turkish Cavalry and Bashi-Bozouks to the edge of their camp.

More is not known, and possibly the account may be an exaggeration, if not an invention.

The military authorities, however, credit the fact of an attack having been made and repulsed.

JAS. BRANT

Consul Brant to the Earl of Clarendon (received October 1)
(Extract)   *Erzeroom, September 5, 1855*
I have the honour to enclose a memorandum, dated the 1st instant, from General Williams, of which he desired me to forward your Lordship a copy. It arrived this evening at sunset.

Enclosure

Memorandum
Kars, September 1, 1855
The most is made of our provisions; the soldier is reduced to half-allowances of bread and meat, or rice

butter; sometimes 100 drachms of biscuit instead of bread; nothing besides. No money. Mussulman population (3,000 rifles) will soon be reduced to starvation. Armenians are ordered to quit the town tomorrow. No barley; scarcely any forage. Cavalry reduced to walking skeletons, and sent out of garrison; Artillery horses soon the same. How will the field-pieces be moved after that?

The apathy of superior officers is quite distressing. We can hold out two months more. What is being done for the relief of this army?

W. F. Williams

Lord Stratford de Redcliffe to the Earl of Clarendon
(received September 19)

My Lord,   *Therapia, September 6, 1855*
In consequence of your Lordship's continued persuasion, as expressed in your despatch of the 16th ultimo, that no part of the supplies destined for the Turkish forces at Kars ever reached that army, if even they ever left Constantinople, I have repeated my enquiries, and the result is the following statement, made by the person whom I principally employed, and who is officially responsible for the correctness of his statements: "I have ascertained that every article demanded by the Commander-in-chief and General Williams, was duly transmitted." My informant was allowed to inspect the official registers. The Seraskier at the same time thinks it possible that the supplies may

not have gone beyond Erzeroom, whither the winter clothing, which was lately applied for, is now being conveyed. The arrival of a reinforcement of Artillerymen in that city has given much satisfaction.

When I saw the Seraskier two days ago, I urged him to send a supply of provisions, if possible, for the army at Kars. He assured me that it would be impossible for the convoy to reach its destination.

STRATFORD DE REDCLIFFE

The Earl of Clarendon to Lieutenant-Colonel Simmons

Sir,   *Foreign Office, September* 7, 1855

The account of the arrangements proposed by Omer Pasha for the relief of the army in Asia, which is contained in your despatch of the 26th ultimo, is inconsistent with subsequent statements which have reached Her Majesty's Government.

In your despatch you report that Omer Pasha reckons upon taking a portion of the Turkish troops from before Sebastopol and replacing them by General Vivian's Contingent. But it appears by a despatch of a later date from General Simpson, that Omer Pasha has given it as his opinion that General Vivian's Contingent would not be fit to take up a position before Sebastopol until next spring; and in consequence of that opinion, and by reason of General Simpson's protest against having the Contingent sent to him, which protest was founded upon Omer Pasha's opinion, Her Majesty's Government have determined that the Contingent shall not go to join the army before Sebastopol.

CLARENDON

Brigadier-General Williams to the Earl of Clarendon
(received October 8)

My Lord,   *Kars, September 7*, 1855

I had the honour of addressing your Lordship on the 1st instant; on the following night we succeeded in getting 1,500 of our starving horses out of the camp and over the mountains, in spite of the blockading Cavalry. We have not yet heard how many of our horses and men fell into the enemy's hands, but from the reports of spies I should think about 150 of all kinds were captured.

The execution of two spies has, in a great measure, broken up the party within our camp which gave the enemy information.

A dangerous amount of desertion took place on the nights of the 4th and 5th instant, but having shot an Infantry and an Artillery deserter, the mischief was arrested. The town and army now know that no spy or deserter shall escape his doom if taken.

We work without cessation on our entrenchments, and, although on short rations, hope to hold out until relieved, and in the meantime confidently look forward to repulse the enemy if he should assault our works.

We have been obliged to destroy many of our Cavalry horses today, in consequence of want of forage for them.

W. F. WILLIAMS

Brigadier-General Williams to the Earl of Clarendon
(received October 25)

(Extract)   *Kars, September* 10, 1855

The Mushir proposes to endeavour to get tonight a messenger through the enemy's videttes; and I avail myself of the opportunity to inform your Lordship that the Russian army and its detachments occupy the positions they did on the 7th. Their Cavalry are now employed in setting fire to the dry grass on which we endeavour to feed our horses, and for which daily skirmishes take place (up to within the range of our long guns).

The weather has become cold, and snow fell on the surrounding hills on the night of the 8th; but after the equinoctial gales we may have two months sufficiently moderate to admit of military operations. I therefore continue the work of adding to our defences. "Trous de loups" have been made round our entrenchments on the heights, which extend more than a mile from Veli Pasha Tabia to the English Tabias; in the meantime the interior line of the town has not been neglected.

In spite of the military executions I informed your Lordship of in my last despatch, desertion to a serious extent occurred last night; I therefore advised the Mushir to disband the regiment of Redif, from which all these desertions have taken place, to put the officers on half-pay, and to distribute the men amongst the companies of the other corps. The sentence was executed this morning, to the astonishment of the officers and soldiers of this unworthy regiment; and I trust we have now struck at the root of the evil, for the general disposition of the garrison is admirable.

Consul Brant to the Earl of Clarendon (received October 8)
My Lord,   *Erzeroom, September* 11, 1855
I have the honour to enclose a copy of a despatch I this day addressed to his Excellency the Viscount Stratford de Redcliffe regarding the position of Kars, and the measures adopted for its relief. I consider them incomplete unless a force be sent up direct to Kars by Trebizond and Erzeroom. I would not wish to throw discouragement on the result of the expedition under Omer Pasha, but I cannot divest my mind of great anxiety as to its result from the effects of the climate, and the nature of the country it will have to traverse in its advance on Tiflis—a country of swamps, woods, and rivers, and of small resources for provisioning an army; possessed by an active enemy like the Russians, I conceive the only chance of success against Tiflis (the safety of the army depends on its success) consists in a rapid march through the country. If the proceedings of Omer Pasha be dilatory, he will lose half his men by sickness and privations, and will effect nothing.

In my opinion a much safer plan would have been to have sent even a smaller force by this route. The expedition has been too long delayed, and by this delay its success has been imperilled. I hope most sincerely that my prevision may prove incorrect; everything depends on the activity and energy of Omer Pasha, and the support he may receive from his own Government. If the latter be not greater than my experience leads me to anticipate, I can feel no confidence in a favourable result, and I cannot help thinking that 10,000 European troops, with 3,000 or 4,000 Cavalry, sent to Kars a month ago by this route, would have effected more than the present expedition, even if it proves as large and as complete as it is reported to be.

JAS. BRANT

Consul Brant to Lord Stratford de Redcliffe

My Lord,   *Erzeroom, September* 11, 1855

I have the honour to inform your Excellency that I received a visit from Saleh Bey, a Miralai of Cavalry, who has just arrived from Kars. He is going on to Constantinople, to represent on the part of the Mushir the dangerous predicament in which the garrison stands, unless immediate and direct succours be sent for its relief. He says that Omer Pasha's army will require a month or more before it can move from the coast, and General Mouravieff may not find it necessary to retire from before Kars for some weeks, and then possibly he will take only his best troops, leaving a sufficient force to maintain the blockade. Now although this force may be small, and the troops not very choice, it will answer the purpose, for the Turkish garrison cannot move a step beyond the entrenchments, because it has no Cavalry, and may be said to be without Artillery, the horses being so reduced in condition that they cannot drag the guns. Thus, while there be any force before Kars, supplied with guns and Cavalry, the garrison cannot venture to issue from its works. The stock of provisions is so small that it will not last until the period arrives when the snow will oblige the enemy to retire to their winter-quarters; so that if succours be not sent up to Kars by Trebizond, without a moment's delay, the garrison may be forced to abandon the place, with the guns and ammunition, and to seek its safety in retreat at any risk.

This is exactly what Saleh Bey stated, and which a letter I saw from Baron Schwartzenburg confirms.

It may happen that General Mouravieff may think it hazardous to leave a small force before the place, not knowing exactly the resources of the garrison, or he may think it necessary to concentrate all his forces to meet the advance of Omer Pasha; still it would be most imprudent to risk the capture of Kars on a matter of opinion as to what General Mouravieff may decide on doing, and therefore the only safe course is to send up to Kars, by way of Trebizond, a sufficient force to oblige the Russians to retire. It might be considered presumptuous in me to say authoritatively what force would suffice, but if I might venture to express an opinion, I should say that 10,000 Infantry and 3,000 to 4,000 Cavalry, all good troops, would effect the purpose. There are guns enough here already. I cannot help feeling that were the troops European the purpose would be effected with more ease and certainty.

The relief of Kars is a matter of too great importance to be treated with indifference or apathy, for besides its being due to its gallant defenders to rescue them from their dangerous position, the loss of the fortress with its guns would seriously increase the difficulties of a future campaign.

I would therefore presume to press on your Excellency the necessity of inducing the Porte to send up, without a moment's delay, a force to relieve Kars, quite independent of Omer Pasha's army. From the usual mode of proceeding of the Turkish Government, it may be apprehended that having dispatched Omer Pasha with a large force, it may consider that it has done all that is required; but if the first effort be not followed up by other prompt and energetic measures, the expedition may prove only an additional disaster, and Kars may still fall.

JAS. BRANT

Brigadier-General Williams to the Earl of Clarendon
(received October 25)

My Lord,   *Kars, September* 14, 1855

Having learnt that the Bashi-Bozouks of Lazistan, now in garrison at Erzeroom, had committed many acts of violence towards the townspeople, I have written by this estafette to Tahir Pasha, the Chief of the Military Medjlis of that city, to enjoin him to repress, with the utmost promptitude and severity, any future similar acts.

From my more recent despatches your Lordship will have perceived that desertion is the great evil against which we have to contend. In spite of the example exhibited to the troops in the disbanding of the regiment of Redif, as detailed in my despatch of the 10th instant, we had no less than six desertions yesterday; fortunately we recaptured two of them; they proved to be men of the corps in question. They were tried by a Council of War, and instantly shot. On their trial they denounced the parties (inhabitants of Kars) who had instigated them to this act of treason, and furnished them with peasants' clothes to enable them to effect their purpose. Three of these men were seized in a house where the musket of one of the prisoners who suffered yesterday was found, together with the clothes and appointments of seven more deserters. There can be little doubt that these wretches are in communication with the enemy, as proclamations were found on the last-captured spy, offering any deserters free passage through the Russian posts to their homes.

A Council of War has tried and condemned these men, who will be hanged today in the marketplace; and the appointments of the seven deserters who have escaped by their agency will be exhibited on the gallows, as a further proof of their guilt.

Your Lordship will learn with pleasure that, up to this moment, no Christian subject of the Sultan has betrayed us, all those who have so justly forfeited their lives being Mussulmans.

With regard to the movements of the enemy, it is impossible for us to obtain any information, except through their deserters. By the deposition of two of them, it would appear that General Mouravieff quitted his camp on the night of the 10th instant, and marched with from twelve to seven battalions in the direction of the Soghanli-Dagh, or Mountain Pass on the Erzeroom road: whether this be for the purpose of attacking Penek and Olti (where the Russian General may suppose that we have collected supplies), or in order to gather the harvest in other districts, cannot, as yet at least, be ascertained; but I have written to Tahir Pasha, at Erzeroom, on the subject, and urged him to procure all the grain within a certain radius round that city.

The health and spirit of our troops are most satisfactory; on the part of the enemy, on the contrary, I believe much sickness to exist.

W. F. WILLIAMS

Lord Stratford de Redcliffe to the Earl of Clarendon
(received September 26)

(Extract)   *Therapia, September* 15, 1855

Anxious, as in duty bound, to co-operate to the utmost of my power towards the relief of the Sultan's army at Kars, I wrote more than two months ago to

Her Majesty's Consul at Bagdad, requesting that he would employ his good offices, in order, if possible, to produce that kind of reliable understanding between the Pasha of the province and the discontented tribes in his vicinity, as might warrant his Excellency in sending a portion of the regular troops at his disposal, if not to Kars, at least in that direction.

The suggestion was little better than a forlorn hope, and Captain Jones's answer reached me only yesterday. I learn from its contents that he sees great objections to the proposed interference, for reasons which he has stated with much frankness, and, as it would seem, with an adequate knowledge of the subject.

Brigadier-General Williams to the Earl of Clarendon
(received October 25)

My Lord,   *Kars, September* 19, 1855
I have the honour to enclose, for your Lordship's information, the copy of a despatch which I have this day addressed to his Excellency the Viscount Stratford de Redcliffe.

W. F. WILLIAMS

Enclosure

Brigadier-General Williams to Lord Stratford de Redcliffe
My Lord,   *Kars, September* 19, 1855
I have the honour to acknowledge the receipt of your Excellency's despatch of the 21st ultimo, conveying

intelligence which, it is needless for me to assure your Lordship, afforded pleasure and imparted hope to all within these entrenchments.

The large force detached from the Russian Army, which I informed your Lordship was operating in the neighbourhood of the Soghanli-Dagh, was seen by my foot-messenger about eight days ago marching in the direction of Penjrood in Geuleh, where Haji Ali Pasha and several other officers who had recently left Kars, were stationed, for the purpose of pasturing the Cavalry and Artillery horses which accompanied them, and for seizing a favourable opportunity to get barley into our camp.

Haji Ali Pasha, with his attendants, having incautiously ventured too far from these detachments, was taken prisoner, and is now in the Russian camp, opposite our entrenchments.

This is the second Pasha who has been taken in this manner, Bahlool Pasha, the hereditary Chief of Byazid, having fallen into the enemy's hands near Euch-Kelissa about two months ago. I should state to your Lordship that by Prince Paskiewitch's official reports on the last war, this very Bahlool Pasha allowed himself to be taken prisoner in Byazid, and whilst in the enemy's hands exerted himself as an active partisan in their favour by intriguing with and rendering neutral several of the Sultan's Koordish subjects.

The similarity of the game played and playing by this man forces me to bring him to your Excellency's notice; the more so, as several of the Koordish bands of Horse under Veli Pasha during the recent unsuccessful operations of the Russian General-in-chief against Erzeroom, disbanded and fled to their homes without firing a shot.

Another very serious coincidence is the conduct of the principal Mussulman inhabitants of Erzeroom during the late panic. There is no doubt that they would have negotiated with the enemy if the forts around the city had not restrained them, and prevented an attack from the Russian army. I can only conclude that, as in 1829, Russian gold was ready at hand to effect its work.

The Christian notables and their flock alone (under their Bishop) showed true loyalty, and I have thanked them, through his Reverence, in the name of the British Government.

Two officers have particularly distinguished themselves since the enemy's army sat down before Kars—Colonel Kadri Bey, of the 2nd Regiment of Anatolia, and Colonel Kadri Bey, of the 6th Regiment of Arabistan. I have consulted with the Mushir, and received his permission to bring the names of these officers to the notice of your Lordship, in order that your influence might be instrumental in obtaining for them the rank of Liva or Brigadier-General.

W. F. WILLIAMS

The Earl of Clarendon to Brigadier-General Williams
Sir,   *Foreign Office, September* 20, 1855
I enclose for your information a copy of a despatch from Viscount Stratford de Redcliffe [dated September

6, 1855], respecting the steps taken to forward supplies for the use of the army at Kars.

CLARENDON

*Lord Stratford de Redcliffe to the Earl of Clarendon
(received October 1)*

My Lord,   *Therapia, September* 20, 1855
On the receipt of the last despatches from Kars and Erzeroom, urging the increased necessity of immediate relief, I addressed a fresh remonstrance, accompanied with strong suggestions, to the Porte, upon that subject.

A copy of my letter, duplicate of which was sent to the Seraskier, is enclosed herewith for your Lordship's information.

STRATFORD DE REDCLIFFE

Enclosure

Lord Stratford de Redcliffe to Fuad Pasha
(Translation)
Sir,   *Therapia, September* 18, 1855
I have just received despatches from Kars and Erzeroom, and I think it my duty to direct your most serious attention to a part of their contents without loss of time.

There is a report that fifteen days ago an attack of the Russians was repulsed by the garrison of Kars; but as your Excellency has received no confirmation of this report, I may be at least permitted to doubt its correctness. What we know for certain is ominous of evil. The army and the garrison begin to feel strongly the effect of their isolation. The provisions are so much diminished, that it has been judged necessary to put the troops on half rations. The horses are attenuated by famine—part of the Cavalry had been obliged to be sent at any risk to the other side of the mountains. The Russians, on the contrary, are reinforcing that arm, and threaten to cut off even the most secret means of communication. In spite of these difficulties, it is of the greatest urgency that no means should be neglected of introducing provisions into the town. Success is not impossible, and the object to be gained is worth the risk. Unhappily the agents, both civil and military, upon whom rests the immediate responsibility, have not up to this time evinced that energy and resolution which circumstances so critical demand. For this reason I address the Porte, through the medium of your Excellency, so that the necessary orders may forthwith be sent from here, and that a vigorous impulse may be given to the authorities at Erzeroom. The delays which have retarded the expedition of Omer Pasha give additional importance to the duties to be performed on the side of Erzeroom.

It wants but five weeks to the winter of that country, and every possible effort ought to be made to provide the troops with the means of prolonging their resistance during that painful interval.

STRATFORD DE REDCLIFFE

Lord Stratford de Redcliffe to the Earl of Clarendon
(received October 8)

My Lord,   *Therapia, September* 26, 1855

In answer to my inquiries at the Porte, I am assured that nothing further has been received from Omer Pasha; that the passage of troops and the conveyance of provisions are in progress, though slowly, in consequence of the limited command of transport for those purposes.

It is impossible not to apprehend that the many changes of plan, the exigencies of our operations at Sebastopol, and heavy demands on the transport service, concur to diminish the hope of relieving Kars.

In reply to my earnest solicitations that a peremptory order should be immediately sent to the commanders at or near Erzeroom to attempt the introduction of provisions into Kars at every risk, I am assured by the Seraskier that orders to that effect are already on the road.

Advices from General Williams to the 7th are not expressive of despair; but the accounts delivered orally at the Porte by an aide-de-camp, dispatched from Kars by Vassif Pasha, represent the danger from want of provisions as very urgent, and I grieve to add that the Turkish Ministers conceive it impracticable to afford any relief in that respect; although it appears that of 1,500 Horse sent out from Kars, only 150, or, according to the Turkish version, 300 and an officer were intercepted by the enemy.

STRATFORD DE REDCLIFFE

Brigadier-General Williams to the Earl of Clarendon
(received October 25)

My Lord,   *Kars, September* 28, 1855

The measures which I detailed in my last despatch have, I am happy to inform your Lordship, entirely put a stop to desertion and conspiracy.

The glorious news of the destruction of Sebastopol and of the Russian fleet reached us four days ago; two royal salutes were fired on the occasion, and the details of these events were read to the troops and the men of Kars, who have throughout our long struggle evinced equal activity and determination. The spirit which reigns within our entrenchments is excellent.

The Mushir has received late news from Omer Pasha, whose army was rapidly concentrating on the Choorooksoo, and who intended to begin his operations against Georgia without a moment's unnecessary delay.

I regret to inform your Lordship that cholera appeared amongst us on the 26th instant; the enemy, I hear and believe, has suffered severely; his camp being so close to us, and on the banks of the Kars-tchai, the river, as usual in these countries, has conveyed the disease to us. Dr Sandwith has taken all necessary measures to prevent the spreading of the evil.

The enemy sent off yesterday about 3,000 loaded arabas or carts to Gumri, and last night lanterns were seen along that road, which, coupled with the displacement of several hospital tents in the great camp, lead me to anticipate a move on the part of the Russian General.

If I can credit the reports of peasants brought in at various times within the last ten days, the enemy has detached (during the night and unperceived by us) a force of 8,000 men towards Ahkiska. This intelligence, however, requires confirmation. Be this as it may, stringent orders will go today to the military and civil authorities of Erzeroom to prepare provisions and land carriage for instant transmission to this garrison, in the event of a retrograde movement on the part of the enemy.

W. F. WILLIAMS

Brigadier-General Williams to the Earl of Clarendon
(received October 25)

My Lord,   *Kars, September* 29, 1855
I have now the honour to inform your Lordship that General Mouravieff, with the bulk of his army, at daybreak this morning attacked our entrenched position on the heights above Kars and on the opposite side of the river. The battle lasted, without a moment's intermission, for nearly seven hours, when the enemy was driven off in the greatest disorder, with the loss of 2,500 dead and nearly double that number of wounded, who were for the most part carried off by the retreating enemy. Upwards of 4,000 muskets were left on the field.

Your Lordship can, without a description on my part, imagine the determination of the assailants and the undaunted courage of the troops who defended the position for so many hours.

The Mushir will doubtlessly at a future moment bring before his Government the conduct of those officers who have distinguished themselves on this day, a day so glorious for the Turkish arms.

On my part I have great gratification in acquainting your Lordship with the gallant conduct of Lieutenant-Colonel Lake, Major Teesdale, and Captain Thompson, who rendered the most important service in defending the redoubts of Veli Pasha Tabia, Tahmasb Tabia, and Arab Tabia. I beg to recommend these officers to your Lordship's protection.

I beg also to name my Secretary, Mr Churchill, an Attaché of Her Majesty's Mission in Persia; he directed the fire of a battery throughout the action, and caused the enemy great loss.

I also beg to draw your Lordship's attention to the gallant bearing of Messrs Zohrab and Rennisson, who as interpreters to Lieutenant-Colonel Lake and Major Teesdale rendered very effective service. Dr Sandwith has been most active and efficient in the management of the ambulances and in the hospital arrangements.

We are now employed in the burial of the dead, and I will have the honour by the next messenger of detailing the movements of this eventful day.

Our loss was about 700 killed and wounded.

W. F. WILLIAMS

Brigadier-General Williams to the Earl of Clarendon
(received October 29)

My Lord,   *Kars, September* 30, 1855

We could not get the messenger out of the lines last night. Today we have repaired our breastworks, filled the tumbrils and replenished the pouches of the Infantry, so that everything, as well as everybody, is ready for the Russians, should they wish to try their fortunes once more.

We have collected, and are now burying the enemy's dead, at least 3,000; round the scenes of especial strife, and in all the camps, they have been firing volleys over those they took away, and who were slain at some distance by round shot; the number of wounded cannot be less than 4,000. If we had only possessed a few hundred Cavalry we should have utterly destroyed their army: their loss in officers has been enormous, and they behaved splendidly; three were killed on the platform of the gun in Tackmas Tabia, which at that moment was worked by Major Teesdale, who then sprang out and led two charges with the bayonet; the Turks fought like heroes, Colonel Lake retook the English Tabias, with the bayonet, too; and Colonel Thompson crushed them with his guns from Arab Tabia.

Such was the deadly fire of our Riflemen (Regular Chasseurs) that 800 dead bodies now lie in front of an épaulement defended by 400 of that arm. I am so fatigued that I can scarcely hold my pen, but I am sure your Lordship will pardon the scrawl. I leave it, as well as my despatch, open for the perusal of the Ambassador.

W. F. WILLIAMS

OCTOBER 1855

The Earl of Clarendon to Lord Stratford de Redcliffe

My Lord,   *Foreign Office, October* 3, 1855

Her Majesty's Government approve of the representation which you made to the Porte, urging the
necessity of immediate steps for the relief of Kars, as
conveyed in your note to Fuad Pasha, of which a copy
is enclosed in your despatch of the 20th ultimo.

CLARENDON

Brigadier-General Williams to the Earl of Clarendon
(received November 8)

(Extract)   *Kars, October* 3, 1855

I had the honour to announce to your Lordship on the evening of the 29th ultimo the glorious victory gained on the morning of that day by the Sultan's troops on the heights above Kars over the Russian army commanded by General Mouravieff, and I now beg to furnish your Lordship with the principal incidents of that sanguinary battle.

Your Lordship will perhaps recollect that in my despatch of the 28th June, I stated that the Russian General, after his second demonstration against the southern face of our entrenchments, which is flanked by Hafiz Pasha Tabia and Kanly Tabia, marched south, and established his camp at Boyouk-Tikmeh, a village situated about four miles from Kars. Knowing that General Mouravieff served in the army which took Kars in 1828, I conceived his last manœuvre to be preparatory either to a reconnaissance or an attack upon the heights of Tahmasb, from whence the Russians successfully pushed their approaches in the year above cited.

Whilst, therefore, the enemy's columns were in march towards Boyouk-Tikmeh, I visited those heights with Lieutenant-Colonel Lake, and, after studying the ground, decided upon the nature of the works to be thrown up; these were planned and executed by Lieutenant-Colonel Lake with great skill and energy. I enclose, for your Lordship's information, a plan made by that officer of the town and its neighbouring heights, which are situated on the opposite side of the river of the Kars-tchai, over which three temporary bridges had been thrown to keep up our communications.

Your Lordship will observe that whilst our camp and magazines in the town were rendered as safe as circumstances would allow, the hills above Kars commanded all, and were therefore the keys of our position.

The entrenchments of Tahmasb being those nearest the enemy's camp, demanded the greatest vigilance from all entrusted in their defence. General Kmety, a gallant Hungarian officer, commanded the division which occupied this eminence; he was assisted by Major-General Hussein Pasha, and my Aide-de-camp, Major Teesdale, who has acted as Chief of the Staff.

Throughout the investment, which has now lasted four months, the troops in all the redoubts and entrenchments have kept a vigilant look-out during the night, and, at their appointed stations, stood to their arms long before daybreak.

In my despatch of the 29th ultimo I informed your Lordship of the arrival of the news of the fall of Sebastopol, and of the landing of Omer Pasha at Batoom. I also acquainted your Lordship with the fact that the Russian General was engaged in sending off immense trains of heavy baggage into Georgia, and showing every indication of a speedy retreat. This in nowise threw us off our guard, and Lieutenant-Colonel Lake was directed to strengthen many points in our extensive and undermanned lines; and amongst other works, the Tabia bearing my name was constructed.

At four o'clock on the eventful morning of the 29th, the enemy's columns were reporting to be advancing on the Tahmasb front. They were three in number, supported by 24 guns; the first or right column being directed on Tahmasb Tabia, the second on Yuksek Tabia, and the third on the breastwork called Rennisson Lines. As soon as the first gun announced the approach of the enemy, the reserves were put under arms in a central position, from which succours could be dispatched either to Tahmasb or the English lines.

The mist and imperfect light of the dawning day induced the enemy to believe that he was about to surprise us; he advanced with his usual steadiness and intrepidity, but on getting within range, he was saluted with a crushing fire of artillery from all points of the line; this unexpected reception, however, only drew forth loud hurrahs from the Russian Infantry as it rushed up the hill on the redoubts and breastworks. These works poured forth a fire of musketry and rifles which told with fearful effect on the close columns of attack, more especially on the left one, which being opposed by a battalion of 450 Chasseurs, armed with Minié rifles, was, after long and desperate fighting, completely broken and sent headlong down the hill, leaving 850 dead on the field, besides those carried off by their comrades.

The central column precipitated itself on the redoubts of Tahmasb and Yuksek Tabias, where desperate fighting occurred and lasted for several hours, the enemy being repulsed in all his attempts to enter the closed redoubts, which mutually flanked each other with their artillery and musketry, and made terrible havoc in the ranks of the assailants; and it was here that Generals Kmety and Hussein Pasha, together with Major Teesdale, so conspicuously displayed their courage and conduct. Lieutenant-General Kerim Pasha also repaired to the scene of desperate strife to encourage the troops, and was wounded in the shoulder, and had two horses killed under him.

The right column of the Russian Infantry, supported by a battery, eventually turned the left flank of the entrenched wing of the Tahmasb defences, and whilst the Russian battery opened on the rear of the closed redoubt at its salient angle, their Infantry penetrated considerably behind our position.

Observing the commencement of this movement, and anticipating its consequences, Lieutenant-Colonel Lake, who had taken the direction of affairs in the English Tabias, was instructed to send a battalion from Fort Lake to the assistance of the defenders of Tahmasb, and at the same time two battalions of the Reserves were moved across the flying bridge, and upon the rocky height of Laz Teppè Tabia. These three reinforcing columns met each other at that point, and, being hidden from the enemy by the rocky nature of the ground, confronted him at a most opportune moment; they deployed, opened their fire, which stopped, and soon drove back, the enemy's reserves, which were then vigorously charged with the bayonet at the same moment when General Kmety and Major Teesdale issued from the redoubts at Tahmasb and charged the assailants. The whole of that portion of the enemy's Infantry and Artillery now broke, and fled down the heights under a murderous fire of musketry. This occurred at half-past 11, after a combat of seven hours.

In this part of the field the enemy had, including his reserves, 22 battalions of Infantry, a large force of Dragoons and Cossacks, together with 32 guns.

Whilst this struggle which I have attempted to describe was occurring at Tahmasb, a most severe combat was going on at the eastern portion of the line called the English Tabias.

About half-past 5 o'clock A.M. a Russian column, consisting of eight battalions of Infantry, three regiments of Cavalry, and 16 guns, advanced from the valley of Tchakmak, and assaulted those small redoubts, which, after as stout a resistance as their unavoidably feeble garrisons could oppose, fell into their hands, together with the connecting breastworks defended by townsmen and mountaineers from Lazistan, whose clannish flags, according to their custom, were planted before them on the épaulements, and, consequently, fell into the enemy's hands; but before the firing had begun in this portion of the field, Captain Thompson had received orders to send a battalion of Infantry from each of the heights of Karadagh and Arab Tabia to reinforce the English lines. This reinforcement descended the deep gully through which flows the Kars river, passed a bridge recently thrown across it, and ascended the opposite precipitous bank by a zig-zag path which led into the line of works named by the Turks Ingliz Tabias—the English batteries. Their arrival was as opportune as that of the reserves directed towards Tahmasb, which I have had the honour to describe in the former part of this despatch; these battalions, joined to those directed by Lieutenant-Colonel Lake, gallantly attacked and drove the Russians out of the redoubts at the point of the bayonet, after the artillery of the enemy had been driven from those lines by the cross fire directed from Fort Lake, and from Arab Tabia and Karadagh by Captain Thompson. This officer deserves my best thanks for having seized a favourable moment to remove a heavy gun from the eastern to the western extremity of Karadagh, and with it inflicted severe loss on the enemy.

After the Russian Infantry were driven from the English redoubts, the whole of their attacking force of Cavalry, Artillery, and Infantry retreated with precipitation, plied with round shot from all the batteries bearing on their columns. During their temporary success, however, the enemy captured two of our light guns, which the mortality amongst our horses, from famine, prevented our withdrawing from their advanced positions. He also carried off his wounded and many of his dead; yet he left 363 of the latter within and in front of these entrenchments; and his retreat occurred at least an hour before the assailants of Tahmasb were put to flight.

During this combat, which lasted nearly seven hours, the Turkish Infantry, as well as Artillery, fought with the most determined courage; and when it is recollected that they had worked on their entrenchments, and guarded them by night, throughout a period extending to nearly four months—when it is borne in mind that they were ill-clothed, and received less than half a ration of bread—that they have remained without pay for 29 months, I think your Lordship will admit that they have proved themselves worthy of the admiration of Europe, and established an undoubted claim to be placed amongst the most distinguished of its troops.

With regard to the enemy, as long as there was a chance of success he persevered with undaunted courage, and the Russian officers displayed the greatest gallantry. Their loss was immense; they left on the field more than 5,000 dead, which it took the Turkish Infantry four days to bury. Their wounded and prisoners, in our possession, amounts to 160, whilst those who were carried off are said to be upwards of 7,000.

As the garrison was afflicted with cholera, and I was apprehensive of a great increase of the malady should this melancholy duty of the burial of the dead be not pushed forward with every possible vigour by our fatigued and jaded soldiers, I daily visited the scene of strife to encourage them in their almost endless task; and I can assure your Lordship that the whole battlefield presented a scene which is more easy to conceive than to describe, being literally covered with the enemy's dead and dying.

The Turkish dead and wour ied were removed on the night of the battle. The dead numbered 362, the wounded 631. The townspeople, who also fought with spirit, lost 101 men.

His Excellency the Mushir has reported to his Government those officers who particularly distinguished themselves—a difficult task in an army which has shown such desperate valour throughout the unusual period of seven hours of uninterrupted combat.

The Earl of Clarendon to Lord Stratford de Redcliffe
My Lord,   *Foreign Office, October* 4, 1855
Brigadier-General Williams has reported to me that great apathy exists amongst the Turkish functionaries at Erzeroom, and that every Pasha and Bey who has been charged with missions from the camp at Kars to Erzeroom, has disappeared from the scene of operations.

I have to state to your Excellency, with reference to these facts, that urgent instructions should be sent by the Porte to the authorities at Erzeroom, directing them to execute the instructions forwarded to them by the Mushir.

CLARENDON

The Earl of Clarendon to Brigadier-General Williams
Sir,   *Foreign Office, October* 4, 1855
I have to state to you that Her Majesty's Government entirely approve your proceedings, as reported in your despatch of the 25th of August.

I have instructed Her Majesty's Ambassador at Constantinople to urge the Porte to send instructions to the authorities at Erzeroom in the sense suggested by you in that despatch.

CLARENDON

Consul Brant to the Earl of Clarendon (received October 25)
(Extract) *Erzeroom, October* 5, 1855
I am anxious not to detain the messenger who carries your Lordship the news of the brilliant repulse of the Russian army in its attack on Kars. I am sure your Lordship will appreciate the services of General Williams and his small band of heroes who have achieved so much under every possible discouragement, and in spite of so much apathy, incapacity, and jealousy on the part of the Turkish military commanders.

Kars was still as closely invested as ever, and it is impossible to say when the Russian General may think fit to retire, though I imagine he will scarce be bold enough to try another assault.

It is a subject of sincere congratulation that the loss on the side of the Turks was so small, and especially so that every European remained unharmed.

Brigadier-General Williams to the Earl of Clarendon
(received November 8)
My Lord, *Kars, October* 12, 1855
Notwithstanding the severe defeat experienced by the enemy, he still blockades us closely, and the

erection of huts in his camp this morning shows that he intends to continue this course.

He knows that all our Cavalry horses and the great majority of the Artillery horses are dead of starvation, and that we cannot take the field; he is also aware that cholera inflicts severe losses on us, which are aggravated by the difficulty we have of burying the horses.

Under these circumstances, I address these few lines to your Lordship, with a hope that such representations may be instantly made to General Omer, to act with vigour and decision against Georgia; otherwise, in spite of our brilliant victory, we must ultimately fall into the enemy's hands.

W. F. WILLIAMS

Lord Stratford de Redcliffe to the Earl of Clarendon
(received October 25)

My Lord,   *Therapia, October* 15, 1855
Immediately on receipt of despatches from Kars announcing the repulse of the Russians with circumstances so highly honourable to all within the walls of that fortress, and more particularly to Brigadier-General Williams, and the British officers and others serving under him, I wrote to congratulate the Porte on so glorious and seasonable a success, expressing a hope that justice would be done to our gallant countrymen by a suitable expression of the Sultan's approval.

I am happy to say that the Turkish Ministers show every disposition to meet my wishes, and to obtain the Sultan's consent to an adequate demonstration in favour of those to whom the victory, under Providence, is principally due.

Copies of the correspondence which passed on the occasion are enclosed herewith for your Lordship's information. Fuad Pasha's letter to me, and my communication to him, crossed each other on the way.

A letter of the 30th ultimo, from Kars, received at Erzeroom, and transmitted in substance to the French Embassy, affirms that the Russian forces, after their defeat, had retired within their cantonments.

STRATFORD DE REDCLIFFE

Enclosure 1

Fuad Pasha to Lord Stratford de Redcliffe
(Translation)

Sir,   *October* 13, 1855

An official report from the General Commandant at Kars, dated 29th of September, announces to us the following news:

The Russians attacked Kars on that day, and the combat lasted eight hours, and during the contest, which was hard fought in the extreme, the enemy entered several times into some of the batteries, from which he was driven back with considerable loss: after displaying unheard-of efforts, the Russians were forced to yield before the courage of our brave soldiers, and to retire completely routed. Besides the dead and wounded carried off during the action, they have left in the trenches and all round the place 4,000 dead, 100 prisoners, and 1 piece of artillery. Our loss is between 700 and 800, amongst whom we have to deplore the death of several superior officers. This magnificent affair covers the besieged army with glory, and adds another laurel to the success of the alliance. The Russians were preparing to retreat, with the intention of raising the siege.

In hastening to bring to the knowledge of your Excellency this welcome news, I avail, etc.

FUAD

P.S. Vassif Pasha makes very honourable mention of General Williams, and congratulates himself on the loyal assistance which that General has given him.

Enclosure 2

Lord Stratford de Redcliffe to Fuad Pasha
(Translation)
Sir,   *October* 13, 1855
In acknowledging the receipt of the letter in which your Excellency has been so good as to communicate to me the welcome news which you have just received from Kars, I have a real pleasure in reiterating the congratulations which I had already expressed when transmitting through M. Pisani the information of the same import which had reached me from General Williams. The brilliant success obtained over the enemy by the Ottoman army is the more worthy

of public rejoicing, as being the result of the loyal and patriotic sentiments which have inspired that army with the determination to dare and suffer everything in a most critical position.

All the allies have just cause to pride themselves upon the victorious bravery which the Imperial troops and the inhabitants of Kars have shown during a deadly conflict of seven hours' duration, and I learn with pleasure from your Excellency, that Vassif Pasha, in his report of the event, has not forgotten how much the brave General Williams and the other officers of my country have contributed to the triumph of his arms both on the ever-memorable 29th of September, and also from the commencement of the siege, and even before the approach of the Russian battalions.

I doubt not that the Government of His Majesty the Sultan will cause the public to participate in the joy which it experiences upon this happy occasion, and I should be too much flattered at the opportunity of adding my feeble tribute to the general manifestations of rejoicing.

STRATFORD DE REDCLIFFE

Consul Brant to the Earl of Clarendon
(received November 8)

(Extract)   *Erzeroom, October* 16, 1855
I have the honour to enclose copy of a despatch I addressed to his Excellency Viscount Stratford de Redcliffe, when forwarding General Williams'

despatch. I sincerely hope his Excellency will induce the Porte, as well to hasten Omer Pasha's movements, as to send troops up hither, and if great expedition be not employed, they may reach too late.

I am greatly disappointed that, notwithstanding the arrival of Omer Pasha in Georgia, and the terrible defeat of the Russian army on the 29th September, General Mouravieff has not withdrawn within the Georgian frontier, and I can only attribute this to his conviction that Omer Pasha will not march on Tiflis this winter, and the certainty that the Kars army cannot molest his, because it has no horses for its Artillery and no Cavalry, and therefore must of necessity remain within its entrenchments.

Enclosure

Consul Brant to Lord Stratford de Redcliffe

(Extract)   *Erzeroom, October* 16, 1855

I have the honour to enclose a despatch sent to me by General Williams to be forwarded to your Excellency, and I hope no time may be lost in relieving the Kars army.

I had hoped that the signal defeat the Russian army met with would have caused its immediate retreat; but it would appear that General Mouravieff still hopes to starve out the garrison.

I learn from the coast that Omer Pasha's army reaches so tardily that there is little chance of its being able to move in advance this winter.

Brigadier-General Williams to the Earl of Clarendon
(received November 29)

My Lord,   *Kars, October* 19, 1855

The enclosed letters, addressed to his Excellency Omer Pasha, will show your Lordship that I took the earliest opportunity of entering into communication with that general officer, but although Batoom, the base of his operations, is but four days' journey from Kars, not a word has been heard, either by the mouth of one of his aides-de-camp, or otherwise, subsequently to the message which I have had the honour to inform your Lordship Omer Pasha sent by one of Vassif Pasha's officers. We are, therefore, totally in the dark with regard to the movements of the relieving army.

I have, on two occasions, had the honour of laying before your Lordship the state of our affairs here, and it is therefore needless for me to say that we will hold out against famine, and resist any future attack of the enemy to the last.

I regret to state that desertion has again commenced, and with it, military executions, for I am determined that no deserter who again falls into our hands shall escape the punishment due to his infamy.

The enemy annoys us much by night alerts, but the spirit of the garrison is admirable, and I am happy to acquaint your Lordship that there has been a sensible decrease of cholera since I last had the honour of writing.

W. F. WILLIAMS

Enclosure 1

Brigadier-General Williams to Omer Pasha

(Translation)

Excellency,   *Kars, October* 2, 1855

Major Mahmood Effendi being about to leave tonight, with despatches from the Mushir of this army, I hasten to seize the opportunity of offering to your Excellency, as Generalissimo of the troops of His Majesty the Sultan, my congratulations upon the glorious victory obtained by this army over the Russians upon the 29th of last month.

His Excellency the Mushir will give you a detailed account of the events of that memorable day. I shall confine myself to observing that the interment of the Russians left dead on the field of battle is continued this morning. More than 4,000 have been already buried. Consequently the losses of General Mouravieff cannot be less than 8,000 men, probably still more, for the number of wounded who escaped from the field of battle on the side of the Russian camp was enormous.

A large convoy of waggons is proceeding at this moment, by the mountain-road opposite, towards Gumri; but the future alone can make known to us the ulterior intentions of the Russian General.

W. F. WILLIAMS

Enclosure 2

Brigadier-General Williams to Omer Pasha

(Translation)

Highness,   *Kars, October* 10, 1855

His Excellency the Mushir intending to send you an express tonight, I take advantage of the opportunity to inform you that the enemy, after having sent off many of his wounded and much of his baggage to Gumri, remains in the position which he occupied previous to the assault, and that even at this moment a convoy (supposed to be of provisions) is in sight coming from the Russian frontier.

This would seem to indicate that General Mouravieff contemplates the continuation of the blockade to which we have now been subjected for more than four months.

Your Highness knows, without doubt, the fact that nearly all our horses, both of the Cavalry and the Artillery, exist no longer, in consequence of the utter want of forage.

W. F. WILLIAMS

Lord Stratford de Redcliffe to the Earl of Clarendon
(received November 1*)*

My Lord,   *Therapia, October* 21, 1855

I have the honour to transmit herewith copies of my latest despatches to Her Majesty's Commissioner at Kars. I take this opportunity to supply an omission which has occurred in my despatch of the 15th instant, and to forward copies of an instruction which I addressed to M. Pisani the moment I heard of the victory of Kars, and of his report in reply to it.

STRATFORD DE REDCLIFFE

Enclosure 1

Lord Stratford de Redcliffe to Brigadier-General Williams
Sir,   *Therapia, October* 19, 1855
I cannot better convey to you the impressions pro-duced, not only on this Embassy, but on the Turkish Government, and indeed on the whole population of Constantinople not devoted to Russia, than by for-warding to you, as I have the honour to do herewith, the correspondence which passed between myself and the Ottoman Secretary of State on the arrival of your despatch of the 29th ultimo, and of those addressed at the same time by Vassif Pasha to the Porte.

I beg to offer both to you and the officers under your command, as well as to the Turkish Commander-in-chief, my cordial congratulations.

I am authorised by the Turkish Ministers to inform you that an officer will be sent on purpose by the Sultan, as soon as circumstances admit of it, to present to you and other officers of Kars those marks of high distinction which His Majesty is in the habit of conferring on such occasions.

STRATFORD DE REDCLIFFE

Enclosure 2

Lord Stratford de Redcliffe to Brigadier-General Williams
Sir,   *Therapia, October* 19, 1855
Referring to what you state in your despatch of the
19th ultimo respecting Bahlool Pasha, I have brought
the circumstances you mention to the knowledge of
the Grand Vizier, and I trust that proper attention will
be paid to the suspicious conduct of that individual.

I am happy to meet your wishes, in so far as it
depends upon me, with respect to the two Colonels
whom you have recommended in the same despatch.

STRATFORD DE REDCLIFFE

Enclosure 3

Lord Stratford de Redcliffe to M. E. Pisani
Dear Sir,   *Therapia, October* 12, 1855
I wish you to wait on the Grand Vizier tomorrow,
and to offer my hearty congratulations on the brilliant success which has been obtained under such
trying circumstances by the Sultan's army at Kars. It
appears that the Russians attacked that place with the
greater part of their forces on the 29th ultimo, and
that, after seven hours' hard fighting, they were compelled to submit in disorder with a loss of 2,500
killed, twice that number in wounded, and 4,000
muskets left on the field. Later accounts state that
they had actually retreated, or were preparing to
retreat, from before the place. I presume that the

Porte has received advices of the same purport from Vassif Pasha.

Orders have been sent to prepare convoys of ammunition and provisions at Erzeroom with a view to the supply of Kars at the earliest possible moment, and I trust that whatever the Porte can possibly do to second the preparations will be done without delay.

So important and glorious a repulse of powerful and well-commanded enemies reflects the highest honour on all concerned, and I have no doubt that His Majesty the Sultan will hasten to encourage the survivors by a signal demonstration of his approval and favour.

With respect to the British officers who have had so large a share in the fatigues, privations, and dangers of the siege, I am convinced that the Porte, of her own accord, will make the acknowledgments due to them. I venture to hope that an officer will be sent direct from the Sultan with His Majesty's gracious acceptance of their services, and such honourable rewards as the occasion appears to require. It will afford me the highest satisfaction to be made the channel of some assurance to this effect.

Read this instruction to the Grand Vizier and to Fuad Pasha.

STRATFORD DE REDCLIFFE

Enclosure 4

M. E. Pisani to Lord Stratford de Redcliffe

My Lord,   *Yenikeuy, October* 13, 1855

I have the honour to report that having read and explained to the Grand Vizier and Fuad Pasha the whole of your Excellency's instructions to me of yesterday's date, respecting the intelligence from Kars, and directing me to offer your hearty congratulations on the brilliant success which has been obtained by the Sultan's army etc. I am requested by the Ministers to thank your Excellency for your friendly and kind congratulations, and to inform you that, as soon as Vassif Pasha's despatches reached the Porte, his Highness lost no time in laying them before the Sultan, accompanied with a report containing suggestions as to the advisability of encouraging the services by a signal demonstration of his Imperial approval and favour: and your Excellency may be assured, added he, that the British officers who so highly contributed to the success of the glorious repulse of the common enemy, will not be forgotten, and their services duly acknowledged.

The Grand Vizier, therefore, authorises your Excellency to give them assurances to this effect. With reference to ammunition and provisions to be sent from Erzeroom for the supply of Kars, the Grand Vizier said that the aide-de camp who brought Vassif Pasha's despatches states that a convoy of 10,000 horses were ready to start with the necessary supplies.

You may depend, observed his Highness, that the Porte, under the management of a Seraskier like Mehmed Rushdi, cannot fail to do its duty, and give satisfaction.

Vassif Pasha praises very highly the services and courage displayed by the inhabitants on this occasion, and recommends that they should be handsomely rewarded. The Porte's intention appears to be, if sanctioned by the Sultan, to exempt them for three years from all direct and indirect taxes.

Et. Pisani

*Brigadier-General Williams to the Earl of Clarendon
(received November 29)*

My Lord,   *Kars, October* 23, 1855
Our courier has been for the four last nights unable to pass the enemy's videttes; he will try again tonight, and I avail myself of the opportunity to state that we heard yesterday of the expedition to Erzeroom, under Selim Pasha, and that I have requested Mr Brant to see that General on his arrival in Erzeroom, and to urge on him my hope that he will use the most energetic means to succour this garrison.

All our horses are dead of starvation, and we have not carriage for a load of ammunition, if we are ultimately obliged to abandon Kars. The garrison has been without animal food for more than a fortnight.

W. F. Williams

Lord Stratford de Redcliffe to the Earl of Clarendon
(received November 7)

My Lord,   *Therapia, October* 24, 1855

Enclosed herewith, for your Lordship's information, is a translated copy of the Sultan's rescript, acknowledging the brilliant successes obtained by the garrison and inhabitants of Kars, more particularly in their repulse of the Russians on the 29th ultimo.

Your Lordship will be glad to observe that the services of General Williams are pointedly acknowledged, by the Sultan's declared intention of sending him the decoration of the Order of Medjidiyé and a sabre of honour.

The British officers serving under General Williams will, no doubt, be severally distinguished, according to their ranks, as soon as their names are sent in by the Commander-in-chief.

It is the Sultan's intention to grant the inhabitants of Kars an exemption from taxes and conscription from the present period till the end of three years after the conclusion of peace.

STRATFORD DE REDCLIFFE

Enclosure

Firman to the Army at Kars

(Translation)

To the Commander of my army in Anatolia, Mehmed Vassif Pasha etc.

Be it known to you on receipt of this Imperial

rescript, you, the above lauded Vizier, that I felicitate you, and together with you, the Feriks, the Emirs, the Zabits, and all the valorous soldiers, on the complete success which has at this time crowned your arms. You have held Kars during four months against an enemy three times your strength; you have displayed the greatest qualities of the soldier in your steadiness, the maintenance of discipline, and in supporting privations, and have all proved yourselves to be endowed with courage.

This quality, moreover, as evinced by you on the 17th of Mouharem, in your resistance to the enemy's attack, is a great subject of glorification to our country and to our race, and it will merit the approbation of the whole world.

You have proved yourselves to be the worthy companions and brothers-in-arms of the brave allies who acquired glorious triumphs in the Crimea, and of the valorous men whose names are illustrated by the siege of Silistria. From the Commander to the private soldier, you have all, as well as the auxiliary Commanders and officers in the service of our army, given full proof of your courage and devotion, and have gained a triumph which will illustrate a great page in the history of the present war, together with your own names. Your services are deserving of my Royal acknowledgment, and you are, all of you, the objects of my constant good wishes.

Those who have laid down their lives in the cause of their country and their race, will ever hold a place in my benevolent recollection. The orphans which they have left I will consider as my own children, and they shall all of them receive proofs of my Royal and special benefaction. All those who have taken a part in this victory shall, in appreciation of their services, receive the honorific medal which I have ordered to be forthwith prepared.

The honour of rewarding the special services of the Commander and superior officers is reflected on the whole army. You, personally, have evinced zeal and ability, as well in commanding the troops as in defending (the place) and conducing to the present triumphant result; and you report that the illustrious Feriks etc., Kerim Pasha, and Williams Pasha, and the Mirliva Pasha, gave especial proofs of devotion and valour. I have, therefore, conferred upon you a sabre enriched with diamonds; upon Kerim and Williams Pashas, the second class of my Imperial order of the Medjidiyé, together with a sabre; and, as a special favour to the Mirliva Pashas and other Emirs and Zabits, to reward those who have given proof of worth and valour, I have ordered to be transmitted to you a set of the distinctive classes of my Imperial order of the Medjidiyé, as well as of the honorific military orders. I appreciate fully the zeal and courage displayed by all the inhabitants of Kars, and the recompense due to them is treated of elsewhere.

The service rendered by you all is deserving of praise and approbation, and in mark of my favour, as well as in grateful appreciation of those services, I have caused the present Imperial rescript to be given from my Royal Divan, and to be sent to you decorated with my sovereign hand.

On receipt of this illustrious decree, you will widely proclaim my Royal pleasure and my satisfaction to all my Emirs, Zabits, and soldiers of the army; and you will use all your endeavours that they should so continue to conduct themselves, in conformity to my Royal wishes, and with their faithful duty, in supporting with devotion and courage the cause of the Empire, so as to increase the Royal favour which I entertain on their behalf.

Be it thus known unto you; and place full reliance on the Imperial cypher.

Given in the middle of the month of Sefer the propitious, in the year 1272.

The Earl of Clarendon to Lord Stratford de Redcliffe
My Lord,   *Foreign Office, October* 26, 1855
With reference to your Excellency's despatch of the 15th instant, I have to inform you that Her Majesty's Government approve of the note which you addressed to Fuad Effendi on the 13th of October, respecting the victory of the 29th ultimo over the Russians at Kars.

CLARENDON

The Earl of Clarendon to Lord Stratford de Redcliffe
My Lord,   *Foreign Office, October* 26, 1855
I have received from Brigadier-General Williams a copy of a despatch which he addressed to your

Excellency on the 19th ultimo, respecting the fidelity and loyalty to the Sultan of the Christians at Kars; and I have to express to you the hope of Her Majesty's Government that you have brought to the knowledge of the Porte, and have recommended for some favourable notice, the good conduct of those Christian subjects of the Sultan, not one of whom appears to have deserted.

CLARENDON

*Lord Stratford de Redcliffe to the Earl of Clarendon
(received November 8)*

My Lord,   *Therapia, October* 29, 1855

I have the honour to forward to your Lordship, herewith, in translation, a copy of the firman by which the Sultan has expressed his sense of the services rendered by the inhabitants of Kars in the late repulse of the Russians from that town.

STRATFORD DE REDCLIFFE

Enclosure

Firman to the inhabitants of Kars

(Translation)

Mehemed Vassif Pasha, Commander of my forces in Asia Minor etc., and Ismail Pasha, Mouteserif of the Sanjak of Kars etc.

Be it known to you, on receipt of this Imperial rescript, that since the beginning of the present war the people of Kars have evinced a good spirit of zeal and devotion. They have thus, from the time that the place was beleaguered by the enemy, shared all the sufferings and the valour of my soldiers. When the enemy assaulted Kars on the 17th of Mouharem, the inhabitants, more particularly, joined my troops with one accord, and devoted their lives to the service of their country. They are co-actors in a triumph that will be recorded in history, and their services are highly appreciated by my Royal person. I shall not only remember them ever with affectionate wishes, but in recompense for their glorious deed, the inhabitants of Kars proper shall, during the war, and for three years after the war, be free from all imposts. Moreover, as they have by this means rendered the military service due by them, the conscription will be dispensed with in favour of the inhabitants of Kars proper during the above period. Those who have distinguished themselves during the war shall be rewarded with nishans, according to their services.

Such is my Imperial will. I have ordered that this exalted rescript, decorated with my Royal hand, should be issued from the Royal Divan, to be proclaimed in evidence of my favour towards the people of Kars.

It is now transmitted to you, the above lauded Mushir and Mouteserif; and you will cause it to be read before the assembly of the whole people; and you will make every one feel how highly my Imperial Majesty appreciates the services rendered by them. You will then cause the same to be inscribed on the records of the Mekhemeh to the glorification of the descendants of all the inhabitants. Hasten to carry out the injunctions of my Royal pleasure.

Be it thus known unto you, and put full credence in the Imperial cypher.

Given in the middle of the propitious month of Sefer, in the year 1272.

Brigadier-General Williams to the Earl of Clarendon
(received November 29)

My Lord,   *Kars, October* 31, 1855

In my despatch of the 3rd instant, in which I had the honour to detail the movements of the battle on the heights of Kars, I omitted to state that the enemy in his retreat left a tumbril on the field.

I have now great pleasure in stating for your Lordship's information that immediately after the battle his Excellency the Mushir, in virtue of the authority with which he is invested by the Sultan, conferred the second class of the Imperial Order of the Medjidiyé on Lieutenant-Colonel Lake for his distinguished services on that day; on Major Teesdale, Captain Thompson, Mr Churchill, and Dr Sandwith, the third class of that Order; and on Messrs Zohrab and Rennisson he bestowed the fourth class.

As these decorations were received in view of the position which their courage and conduct so materially assisted in defending, I trust that your Lordship will obtain Her Majesty's gracious permission to accept and wear them.

His Excellency the Mushir has also named Colonel Lake a General of Brigade in the Turkish army, Major Teesdale a Lieutenant-Colonel, and Captain Thompson a Major in that army; and his Excellency assures me that he has written for the confirmation of those ranks so honourably won by the officers in question.

W. F. WILLIAMS

NOVEMBER 1855

The Earl of Clarendon to Lord Stratford de Redcliffe

My Lord,   *Foreign Office, November* 1, 1855

I have to state to your Excellency that Her Majesty's Government approve of the correspondence of which copies are enclosed in your despatch of the 21st ultimo, and having reference to the late victory at Kars.

The mode of rewarding the inhabitants of Kars for their good conduct on this occasion, and which the Porte seems, from M. Pisani's report, to be disposed to adopt, namely, that of exempting them from taxation for three years, appears very judicious and likely to stimulate the people of other places to similar exertions.

CLARENDON

The Earl of Clarendon to Brigadier-General Williams

Sir,   *Foreign Office, November 2*, 1855

I have received your despatch of the 29th of September last, announcing that General Mouravieff, with the bulk of his army, had at daybreak that morning attacked your entrenched position on the heights above Kars, and on the opposite side of the river, and that after an engagement which lasted nearly seven hours, the enemy was driven off in the greatest disorder and with considerable loss.

I beg to congratulate you upon this brilliant and important victory, which reflects the highest credit upon the garrison of Kars.

It is my agreeable duty to convey to you, and to the British officers under your command, the cordial approbation of the Queen and of Her Majesty's Government, for the energy, the perseverance, and the valour with which, for many months, and under circumstances of extraordinary difficulty, you have laboured with Lieutenant-Colonel Lake, Major Teesdale, and Captain Thompson, together with Mr Churchill and Dr Sandwith, to sustain the spirit and discipline of the Turkish troops, and to place the defences of Kars in a state to resist successfully the attack of the Russian army.

I shall not fail to recommend these officers to the Queen for the rewards due to their gallantry.

CLARENDON

The Earl of Clarendon to Lord Stratford de Redcliffe
My Lord,   *Foreign Office, November* 3, 1855
I enclose, for your Excellency's information, a copy of a despatch [dated November 2, 1855] which I have addressed to Brigadier-General Williams, conveying to him and to the British officers under his command the cordial approbation of the Queen and of Her Majesty's Government of their conduct during the operations at Kars.

CLARENDON

Lord Stratford de Redcliffe to the Earl of Clarendon
(received November 19)
(Extract)   *Therapia, November* 4, 1855
In addition to the Sultan's approval of the conduct of his army at Kars, His Majesty's principal Ministers have addressed a letter of congratulation and thanks to the defenders of that fortress; a translation of the letter in question is enclosed herewith for your Lordship's information.

Enclosure

Address from the Porte to the defenders of Kars

The signal victory which you have gained by the grace of God, and under the auspices of His Majesty the Sultan, is an event which will fill a bright page in history. The courage and valour displayed on this occasion by your Excellency, the officers and soldiers of the Sultan's army under your command, and by the inhabitants of Kars, are deserving of universal praise. They have been duly appreciated by His Imperial Majesty, who has graciously extended his Royal favour towards yourself, the army under your command, and the people of Kars, in reward of the brilliant service rendered by them.

The sufferings undergone by the Imperial forces beleaguered in Kars have troubled the sleep and repose of all of us, and we have never ceased to pray for their safety and success. We were conscious of the zeal and intrepidity which animated your Excellency, and of the infinite mercy of God, and found consolation in this reflection. On the other hand, we worked day and night in devising means to oblige the enemy to raise the siege, and the joyful tidings of this victory has infused new life into us. Such a service rendered to our gracious Master is a glory to the state and to the nation, and His Majesty has permitted that we likewise, as companions, should offer our thanks and congratulations to our brethren, who have been made worthy of so great a victory. We, therefore, from the bottom of our hearts, offer our warm thanks and congratulations to your Excellency, and all the officers and troops of the army, our brothers; and by that you will convey the same to all of them, with our prayers for their prosperity and salvation.

Consul Brant to the Earl of Clarendon
(received December 6)

(Extract)   *Erzeroom, November* 11, 1855

I have the honour to transmit your Lordship a message from the Mushir at Kars to his Excellency Selim Pasha, received yesterday afternoon, which General Williams desired me to communicate to your Lordship, as well as to Viscount Stratford de Redcliffe and Sir James Simpson:

> Our affairs are desperate. Let Selim Pasha's force, with that of Veli Pasha, excepting those intended to garrison the forts of Erzeroom, march upon Kars immediately. Let Mehmet Pasha seize and put at the disposal of the Military Pashas the whole land-carriage of the country. If Selim Pasha has not arrived, let Tahir Pasha send him an express instantly with this message.

I invited Tahir Pasha to come to my house, which he politely did, and there met Majors Stuart and Peel, and Captain Cameron; and after consultation it was agreed that his Excellency should at once visit the Mushir, and urge him to hasten the departure of his force. Early this morning all the British officers waited on the Mushir, who promised, that on the 13th he would march to Kupri-Keuy, and that his further movements would be guided by those of the Russian Byazid Division. The Mushir will have with him a force of about 5,000 Infantry, 2,000 Cavalry (Regulars 1,500, and 500 Irregulars), with 24 guns. His inclination seemed to be to give battle to the Russian Division, which being only 3,000 strong with 6 small guns, his Excellency hoped to defeat, and afterwards to march on Kars. I must say that Selim Pasha has been very dilatory since his arrival, and seemed little disposed to advance at all until the troops promised him by the Seraskier should have arrived; but Major Stuart has, after much persuasion, brought him to his present resolution, as the necessity of the Kars garrison admitted of no delay, and the arrival of the promised troops seems very remote and uncertain, as they have not yet reached Trebizond. I hope the Mushir will follow up his present resolve, and if he will be guided by Major Stuart, I trust a diversion will be made to enable provisions to be introduced to Kars, by the Russians concentrating their troops so as to be prepared for a threatened attack of the army of Selim Pasha.

Consul Brant to the Earl of Clarendon
(received December 6)

My Lord,   *Erzeroom, November* 12, 1855
Yesterday afternoon I received from Kars a despatch from General Williams, who directed me to send a copy to your Lordship, to Viscount Stratford de Redcliffe, and to Sir James Simpson:

Kars, October 3, 1855

I have told the English officers to join Selim and Veli
Pashas in their advance. The enemy came today with 12
battalions and 2 batteries, and 500 carts, to destroy the
village of Shorak, and carry off the wood of the houses.
He was driven out by our Artillery with loss; he set fire
to it, and withdrew. Urge on the relieving army, and also
increase activity in sending troops from Constantinople.
The enemy has struck his tents, and hutted his army.

The village of Shorak was under the Tahmasb Tabia,
and the danger of the enemy's attempt, and his want of
wood, either for firing or for sheltering his troops, may
be guessed by the large force employed. The troops
expected to join Selim Pasha are very slow in their
movements, although the Mushir declares he has notice
of their embarkation at Constantinople from the
Seraskier Pasha; no information of their arrival at
Trebizond has been received. The Russians hutting their
troops, indicates the severe cold in tents, and, possibly,
either their wish to be prepared for a hasty retreat, or
their determination to remain where they are for a longer
period. It would be difficult to divine their true motive,
but I would fain hope it may not be the last; for if so, the
garrison will eventually be forced to yield to famine.

The season has singularly favoured the Russians,
by the snow and bad weather coming so late this year,
but I think it cannot be delayed under any circumstances beyond the end of this month.

JAMES BRANT

Lord Stratford de Redcliffe to the Earl of Clarendon
(received November 29)

My Lord,   *Therapia, November* 19, 1855

I avail myself of today's messenger to forward to your Lordship the substance of a despatch from Brigadier-General Williams dated the 6th instant.

A previous despatch from the same officer dated the 23rd ultimo, and received only two days ago, was immediately communicated by my direction to the Turkish Ministers, who assert that Selim Pasha is authorised to attempt the relief of Kars. Supposing the instructions to have reached him, he is probably acting at this moment in obedience to their tenor.

STRATFORD DE REDCLIFFE

Enclosure

Consul Brant to Lord Stratford de Redcliffe

My Lord,   *Erzeroom, November* 6, 1855

I have the honour to inform your Excellency that I received this morning a despatch from General Williams, the contents of which he desired me to communicate to your Excellency.

The General says: "I have on my shoulders the management of the starving population, as well as that of the army. I take from the rich, and give to the poor, but am now obliged to issue corn from the public stores. I hope Omer Pasha is at least acting like a brave and resolute man. The enemy showed his diminished army yesterday, 16 battalions from 400 to

500 each, 3 regiments of Dragoons, 3 of Cossacks, and 40 guns."

JAMES BRANT

Major Simmons to the Earl of Clarendon
(received December 18)

(Extract)   *Camp on the Sieva, November* 19, 1855

I have to inform your Lordship that the army broke up from Zugdidi on the 15th instant, on which day the communications were opened between the advanced guard at Chopi and Redoute-Kaleh, where Omer Pasha has formed depôts for provisioning the troops. The distance from Redoute-Kaleh to Chopi is about 18 miles, along a road in great measure macadamised, and, consequently, the provisioning of the troops will be much facilitated.

The advanced guard is now at Senaki on the Tikour, the main body being at the village of Taklit (marked Seklami on the map) on the River Sieva. The army is now detained whilst provisions are being brought up from Redoute-Kaleh, and a dêpot formed here, the distance from the sea being about 30 miles.

As soon as this depôt shall be formed, probably in two days, Omer Pasha proposes collecting his army which is now écheloned along the road from the Tikour to Zugdidi, and then moving on again *en masse*.

The troops have been écheloned in this manner to facilitate their provisioning. In the meantime a reconnaissance has been pushed on to the Tkeniss

Zkhal which separates Mingrelia from Immeritia; and it appears that the Russians have entirely evacuated this province. In their retreat they have destroyed all the bridges, and even large culverts on the road; they have abandoned several positions temporarily fortified, and especially the position of this camp, where there is a strong entrenchment which was thrown up last year, covering a large extent of ground and naturally of great strength.

In it were enclosed temporary barracks and a depôt of provisions. Both have been destroyed by fire, as also have a range of temporary barracks at Chopi, and considerable magazines and stores at Cheta, and at Senaki on the Tikour.

In fact, the farther the Turkish army penetrates the country, the more evident it is that the Russians have miscalculated their powers of resistance; and the results of the success of the 6th instant become more apparent. Their losses on that occasion must have been great, and may be moderately estimated at from 1,600 to 1,800 killed and wounded.

I am happy to inform your Lordship that the very strict measures taken by Omer Pasha to prevent pillage have met with great success. The Abassians, who at first caused so much fear to the inhabitants of Mingrelia, and had commenced committing great havoc amongst them, stealing even children, have been sent back into their own country, some of them after receiving severe chastisement from the Turkish military authorities. The few Circassians that remain are held in check; and as to the troops themselves, I do not think, although they have generally found the villages deserted, the whole army have plundered to the value of ten pounds, and to that extent only in articles of consumption. The result is, that as the army advances in the country the villages are less deserted; and I do not despair of the army even deriving some little benefit from the resources of the country: these, however, are not numerous, and will be confined to hay and Indian corn for the horses, and a small sup-ply of meat with some few bât-horses [packhorses]. The country, however, as the army proceeds to the eastward, improves and becomes more cultivated.

I have to inform your Lordship that, according to reports received, the Russians in retiring have burnt their gun-boat flotilla on the Rhion. In fact, every-thing appears to indicate now their inability to resist for any length of time on this side of Kutais. It is not improbable, however, that in order to gain time for the removal of their sick and stores, they may oppose the passage of the Tkeniss-Zkal.

I would farther observe to your Lordship that this army, which numbers in all about 40,000 men, will require strong available reinforcements, if they are to maintain their position at or in front of Kutais, against the Russian army, after it shall be reinforced by Mouravieff's army from before Kars.

The Turkish General, as his army is at present dis-posed, has not much more than 20,000 men to meet the enemy in an advanced position.

He has been able to make no use of the force of 10,000 men which formed the army of Batoom, under Mustafa Pasha, before the diversion in favour of the army of Kars was in contemplation, that force being very much disorganised by mismanagement and weakened by disease. Some little has been done to re-establish it, and probably 6,000 men may be counted upon from it in the spring. The remainder of Omer Pasha's army consists of 16,000 men from before Sebastopol, and 15,000 men from Roumelia, strong detachments of whom it has been necessary to leave to protect the magazines at Soukoum-Kaleh and Tchimshera, to hold Zugdidi and to maintain the communications of the army, so that when the army reaches Kutais it will not much exceed 20,000 men.

If, as has been reported, General Mouravieff has broken up from before Kars, and is on the march to reinforce General Mukrainsky, in Immeritia, the Russian General will have the superiority of force, and it may be expected that the Turkish forces, unaided, will not be able to maintain their position. This union, however, of the Russian forces cannot be expected to take place before the spring.

With reference to the measures to be taken for carrying on the war next spring, I feel convinced that as the results which have hitherto been obtained here are to be attributed to the presence of the troops which Her Majesty's and the French Governments consented to being brought from before Sebastopol, so they can only be maintained and brought to a more successful issue by forming a considerable corps of reserve from the Turkish troops which have already served in Roumelia or the Crimea, under the command of Omer Pasha.

Consul Brant to the Earl of Clarendon
(received December 14)

My Lord,   *Erzeroom, November* 20, 1855

I have the honour to enclose a copy of a despatch which I addressed yesterday to his Excellency the Viscount Stratford de Redcliffe.

Major Stuart and myself have done all we could to urge Selim Pasha to advance, but I fear he is too timid, and wants only a pretext to delay here.

The Kars garrison is in imminent danger, and I am really afraid it must surrender. I am apprehensive Omer Pasha will not advance rapidly enough, and General Mouravieff seems determined to hold out as long as possible. The season favours him signally.

I am in a great state of anxiety, for bravery and skill will soon be unavailing, and they cannot stand out against famine.

JAMES BRANT

Enclosure

Consul Brant to Lord Stratford de Redcliffe

(Extract)   *Erzeroom, November* 19, 1855

I have the honour to inform your Excellency that a peasant from Kars brought me today a few lines from General Williams of the 12th.

The General evidently seems to be in the belief that Selim Pasha has received the troops promised, of whose arrival at Trebizond, however, we have heard nothing, and his Excellency has requested both Major Stuart and myself to entreat your Excellency to hasten their expedition. A Colonel arrived with a long letter from his Excellency Vassif Pasha to Selim Pasha. The precise contents of this letter I do not know, but the object was to urge on his Excellency to the relief of the garrison. Selim Pasha inspected his troops yesterday, and they mustered between 5,000 and 6,000 Infantry: most of the Cavalry were on duty at the outposts; they will amount to nearly 2,000, chiefly Regulars, and besides these, they could collect 1,500 to 2,000 Bashi-Bozouks, if not more. The troops are in good health, well armed and clothed, and have lately received four months' pay, and I have no hesitation in saying that such a force under an active and brave General could relieve Kars; but I have seen enough of Selim Pasha to have discovered that he is neither active nor energetic, nor brave; and I have long feared that he would not advance. He has a new excuse for delay every day; today it was, that he must wait a change of weather: it is much finer than we had any reason to expect at this season, beautifully clear, though a little cold at night, and I can only say that as finer weather cannot be expected before next summer, it is evident his Excellency will not leave Erzeroom. Selim is superior in rank to Vassif Pasha, and will not therefore obey his orders. The former's character was well known from his conduct in the command of the Choorooksoo army, which by neglect he allowed to perish, and yet in circumstances which demand immediate action, a slow and indolent Mushir like him is sent up. It really makes me fear that the Seraskier has no wish or intention of saving from destruction General Williams and his little band of heroes. I would therefore once more earnestly entreat your Excellency to see that a General of character be sent up, with at least a few good troops, with positive orders that they must arrive here in 20 or 25 days, and that every assistance the country can furnish, be afforded to effect this. If a proper man be not at hand, the Porte had better avail of the services of General Cannon and his staff, who are at Trebizond; but should the General be sent, your Excellency must insist that he have the absolute and uncontrolled command of this division, and that not one hour be lost in coming to a decision. The Russians cannot have many troops before Kars, I should think not more than 12,000, and they are discouraged, and have no heart to fight; but in the camp it is said that General Mouravieff is of so obstinate a character, that he will never abandon the siege, even though he should risk his own life, and the destruction of his whole army, by a desperate assault, or by frost or famine. He has put his troops into huts which are well constructed and having plenty of firewood, they can stand the frost for some time yet, and too long, alas! for the safety of the garrison of Kars, which in the last extremity can do nothing but surrender; for without Cavalry, and without horses for their guns, they could never, I imagine, cut their way through the enemy, who is still superior in numbers, taking into account his numerous Cavalry and Artillery.

Omer Pasha is too slow in his movements to hope anything from him. About twelve days ago, his Excellency was still on the coast, and although he had gained a victory, I suppose he will require time before he can resume his advance.

I ask your Excellency, is the Kars army to be allowed to perish? Is nothing to be done to relieve it? For all that the Porte has lately done, is quite insufficient for the purpose. I before pointed out that Omer Pasha's army should have been directed on Kars by way of Erzeroom, and not on Georgia, and had that been done Kars might long since have been saved. I now fear it must surrender, and to confer honours on its gallant defenders, while they be left to perish is a cruel mockery, and an indelible disgrace to the Turkish Government, as well as to those of the allied Powers.

The Earl of Clarendon to Lord Stratford de Redcliffe

My Lord,   *Foreign Office, November* 21, 1855
With reference to your Excellency's despatch of the 4th instant, I have to state to you that Her Majesty's Government concur with your Excellency as to the character of the letter which the Sultan's Ministers have addressed to the defenders of Kars.

The neglected garrison of Kars will at least have the satisfaction of knowing that their sufferings troubled the sleep and repose of the Turkish Ministers, who, in default of all ordinary measures of relief, never ceased to pray for their safety and success.

CLARENDON

Consul Brant to the Earl of Clarendon
(received December 21)

(Extract)   *Erzeroom, November* 24, 1855

I have the honour to inform your Lordship that messenger after messenger has reached me for several days past from General Williams, pressing for succours. I have received short notes from him of the 12th, 13th, and 16th, all to this purport.

Today a despatch came in, of which, by General Williams' desire, I have the honour to send to your Lordship a copy; I experienced the most painful feelings on perusing its contents. That after so gallant a defence, Kars should fall into the hands of a thrice-beaten enemy, on account of the apathy of the Porte and the cowardice and imbecility of Selim Pasha, is intolerably distressing; but the consolatory feeling remains that, however disgrace may attach to those parties whose duty it was to have prevented this melancholy termination of so glorious a struggle, the brave garrison, and the inimitable director of its energies and operations, will to the last maintain their character for valour, skill, foresight, and every soldierly virtue, and that while noble deeds are appreciated, the defence of Kars will stand prominent among the achievements of a war unsurpassed by any other in acts of daring gallantry.

Major Stuart has repeatedly waited on Selim Pasha and has in urgent terms entreated him to advance to the relief of Kars; the Major has done so again today, but met with the same coolness and refusal. His Excellency will neither attempt the relief of the place, nor will he advance to cover the retreat of the garrison, and refuses even to send a strong detachment of Cavalry towards Kars, which the Major and his officers offered to accompany in the hope of rendering assistance to the retiring army.

Selim Pasha now pretends that he fears danger to Erzeroom from the Byazid division and talks of advancing to attack it, but this is a mere pretext to cover his cowardice. I fear there is nothing to be done to help this neglected army: a retreat without Cavalry or Artillery in face of an enemy who commands a large number of both, seems inevitable, and I tremble for the result.

Omer Pasha is too distant and seems too slow in his movements to hope anything from him; and hence all relief is denied: the garrison therefore has nothing to depend upon but its own bravery, and the unflinching resolution, the consummate prudence and skill of its gallant Commander and his heroic band of European officers. Had Selim Pasha not been sent up hither something might have been effected. Veli Pasha would have probably not attempted more than Selim Pasha himself, but if the command had been given to Tahir Pasha, which, without the presence of Selim Pasha, it was in the power of Vassif

Pasha to have ordered, I think relief could have been got into Kars. But as soon as Selim Pasha arrived, all control over the troops here was taken out of Vassif Pasha's hands.

The reputation of Selim Pasha might have led to the anticipation of what has happened; he was so well known as wanting in military knowledge and courage, as well as in administrative talent, that the Seraskier Pasha who named him should be made responsible for the incapacity of his protégé, and Selim Pasha should not be allowed to escape the punishment due to his cowardice and heartless conduct.

Enclosure

Brigadier-General Williams to Consul Brant
Kars, November 19, 1855

Tell Lords Clarendon and Redcliffe that the Russian army is hutted now and takes no notice of either Omer or Selim Pashas. They cannot have acted as they ought to have done. We divide our bread with the starving townspeople. No animal food for seven weeks. I kill horses in my stable secretly, and send the meat to the hospital, which is now very crowded. We can hold out, and try to retreat over the mountains *via* Olti. Have provisions sent in that direction, before the 18th day after this date. We shall carry three days' biscuit with us.

Lord Stratford de Redcliffe to the Earl of Clarendon
(received December 6)

My Lord,   *Therapia, November* 26, 1855

The day before yesterday I received despatches from Kars, Erzeroom, and Trebizond. The substance of them in every essential point is contained in the accompanying abstract. I lost no time in bringing them to the knowledge of the Turkish Ministers. My instruction to M. Pisani is enclosed herewith. I requested General Mansfield also to lend his assistance. The result of his conversation with the Seraskier Pasha is contained in a report of which copy is transmitted herewith for your Lordship's information. An extract of M. Pisani's report is added.

Your Lordship will observe with satisfaction that Omer Pasha's movements are more promising than the accounts from Trebizond allowed me to suppose.

Your Lordship will also take note of what fell from the Turkish Ministers respecting Colonel Stein and Mustafa Pasha.

I had already applied to Admiral Grey for means of transport, and he had undertaken to embark 1,200 or 1,400 troops for Trebizond, and five companies at the Dardanelles, but the horse transports are all employed for our own Cavalry.

I hasten now to resume my application in favour of the Egyptian Infantry at Eupatoria, and I have sent Lord Napier to propose to M. Thouvenel that we should join in placing a large advance from the Loan Fund at the immediate disposal of the

Turkish Government under proper securities as to its application.

The difficulties of which the Seraskier made mention to General Mansfield appear to have resulted from the slowness of the preliminary communications announced by the Porte as preparatory to the meeting of the Commission.

STRATFORD DE REDCLIFFE

Enclosure 1

Lord Stratford de Redcliffe to M. E. Pisani

Sir,   *Therapia, November* 24, 1855.

I send you herewith an abstract of news from Kars, Erzeroom, and Trebizond.

You will lose no time in communicating the contents to Fuad Pasha, the Grand Vizier, and the Seraskier, and you will repeat yet once more my urgent demand that whatever it is possible to do to afford an additional chance for the delivery of Kars and its brave garrison, should be attempted without a moment's delay. Express at the same time the regret which I feel at the apparent inefficiency of Omer Pasha's movements, at his neglecting to communicate by Batoom with Kars, at the confidence which he has placed in Ferhad Pasha, and at his continued toleration of Mustafa Pasha. You will earnestly implore the Turkish Ministers to do whatever may still depend upon those to remedy these crying evils.

I hope that Admiral Grey has been able to comply with the Seraskier's request for transport. You had better communicate with that officer, and ascertain the result of my application to him.

STRATFORD DE REDCLIFFE

P.S. I write to General Mansfield that he may afford you the advantage of his advice and co-operation.

Enclosure 2

Abstract of news from Kars, Erzeroom, and Trebizond
Therapia, November 24, 1855

News from Kars to November 3rd; from Erzeroom to November 12th; from Trebizond to November 17th.

Kars: Russians with 12 battalions, 2 batteries, and 500 carts, had tried to destroy the village of Shorak, for the sake of the wood. They were driven off by the artillery from Tahmasb Tabia, but burnt the village first. The Russians were hutting their troops. Weather favourable to them. Garrison of Kars in great distress. Earnest demands for an advance from Erzeroom, and reinforcements from Constantinople.

Erzeroom: Complaints of the slowness of troops expected from Constantinople, and of Selim Pasha.

Kars: Vassif Pasha writes—"Our affairs are desperate." Forces of Selim Pasha and Veli Pasha, excepting garrisons, ordered to march for Kars, with all the land carriage of the country.

Erzeroom: The Mushir had promised the British officers, who urged him to move with 5,000 Infantry and 2,000 Cavalry, and 24 guns, against the Russian division of 3,000, and 6 guns, to give battle, produce a concentration in forces and get provisions into Kars.

Kars: Loud complaints of not having heard from Omer Pasha for many weeks, though four days takes a foot messenger from Batoom.

Ferhad Pasha has written these words to Kerim Pasha—"On Vassif Pasha will fall all the disgrace of Williams Pasha's acts."

Trebizond: Omer Pasha had found Zugdidi strongly fortified, and was in consequence marching towards Redoute-Kaleh. The Russians had carried off 3,000 head of sheep from Mustafa Pasha's division, and attacked a Circassian village, massacring the inhabitants.

Enclosure 3

Extracts from M. E. Pisani's Reports
Pera, November 25, 1855

In pursuance of your Excellency's instruction of yesterday's date, I lost no time in communicating to Fuad Pasha, the Grand Vizier, and the Seraskier Pasha, the "abstract of news" from Kars, Erzeroom, and Trebizond, and have the honour to report the result of my interview with those Ministers.

With reference to the intelligence contained in the abstract enclosed in your Excellency's instruction, both the Porte and the Seraskier received similar accounts, with the exception, however, of the last paragraph caught from the letters from Trebizond.

The foot messenger who brought the letters from Kars says that the Russian troops had made up their minds to abandon the siege of Kars, when they received intelligence from an Armenian inhabitant of the place that the Turks had hardly fifteen days' provisions; the Russian General thought it worth his while to continue the siege. Meanwhile the traitor, said the messenger, was summarily tried and hanged.

In a council which was held the night before last at the Grand Vizier's residence, it was decided that 8,000 men out of the 12,000 forming the Egyptian division at present at Eupatoria, will be forthwith embarked for Trebizond on their way to Erzeroom; and the Porte wishes to ascertain whether the British Admiral Commanding-in-chief can spare one or two steamers to keep them in conveying a portion of the said division to its destination. A similar application will also be made to the French Embassy.

All this, said his Highness and Excellency, requires money for its execution. The Treasury is much embarrassed, and unless 100,000 purses or 50,000,000 piastres are paid them on account, out of the loan, every operation must be stopped. Omer Pasha demands money, Vassif Pasha likewise, and the Commander at Eupatoria. Besides, the grain merchants and others refuse to give provisions unless they be paid ready money. Under these circumstances, both the Grand Vizier and Fuad Pasha urgently beg of your Excellency to be so good as to take their demand into due consideration, and issue orders to the proper quarter.

The Seraskier Pasha told me that he wrote to Omer Pasha some time back about Ferhad Pasha and that he will write to him again. His Excellency himself is not at all pleased with that man. As to Mustafa Pasha he thinks it proper to inform you, that before Omer Pasha's arrival at Redoute-Kaleh, Mustafa Pasha had applied and obtained leave to go for a change of air to Trebizond, where he had already gone; and subsequently he was to come to Constantinople, when Omer Pasha sent one of his aides-de-camp with a letter ordering Mustafa Pasha to join him. He obeyed the order against his inclination. At all events the Seraskier will endeavour to persuade Omer Pasha to send him to Constantinople. M. Thouvenel also made representations against Mustafa Pasha's remaining there.

Enclosure 4

Brigadier-General Mansfield to Lord Stratford de Redcliffe
My Lord,   *Pera, November* 25, 1855
On the receipt of your Excellency's note of yesterday with its enclosure, I called on M. Pisani, and arranged to accompany him to the Seraskier this morning at an early hour.

We found his Excellency very unwell, but able to attend to business. He had received intelligence regarding the state of things similar to that communicated to your Excellency. He exonerated Omer Pasha from blame and explained his position; the account of his Excellency differing essentially from what has been conveyed to your Excellency in that respect. On the 17th instant Omer Pasha's first division marched on Zugdidi. It was to be followed by a second one immediately. According to the report of Ahmed Pasha, the Admiral on the coast, to the Captain Pasha, the Generalissimo was now actually established at that place. This report was actually a day or two later than the last news from Omer Pasha. The latter had sent a squadron of Cavalry to Redoute-Kaleh from Zugdidi. This probably accounts for the report that he was marching on that road, whereas only a partial movement or reconnaissance had taken place.

Hassan Pasha had marched from Redoute-Kaleh with three or four battalions on the road towards Kutais, and had occupied the entrenchments three hours distant from that place, so long held by the enemy and now found to be evacuated, in consequence of the flank movement of Omer Pasha from Soukoum-Kaleh on Zugdidi.

At the same time Mustafa Pasha had left Batoom and had actually reached Ozurgheti by the date of the last report. Thus there are now three columns, that of Omer Pasha at Zugdidi, that of Hassan Pasha from Redoute-Kaleh, and that of Mustafa Pasha from Batoom, executing a movement of concentration on Kutais.

Omer Pasha has written urgently, requiring that every available transport horse shall be sent to him. Upon the arrival of such animals depends his ability to move forward strongly. The report of Ahmed Pasha is confirmed by that of the Captain of the steamer which arrived yesterday.

A Council of Ministers sat last night.

Full powers have in consequence been sent to Selim Pasha, the Mushir at Erzeroom, to do whatever can be achieved for the relief of Kars.

There are now at Constantinople, ready to sail to Trebizond, 850 riflemen and 120 gunners. These men embark tomorrow in an English steamer hired by the Seraskier for the purpose at 250,000 piastres, as that to be furnished by Admiral Grey will not be ready till Thursday the 29th instant. In the last 25 days, including the above-mentioned men, reinforcements to the amount of 4,000 men will have sailed from Trebizond, to be pushed on at once to strengthen Selim Pasha, who received a fortnight ago stringent orders to attack the Russians posted at Yenikeuy on the road to Kars.

In short, everything has been done that is possible with the means at hand. The old soldiers have all been taken away from the guard-houses at Constantinople and sent towards the seat of war, their places being filled up by recruits.

Marshal Pélissier having proposed that the Turkish troops should be sent from Eupatoria to Varna to winter, the Government of the Sultan had determined to send from thence 8,000 Egyptian Regulars to Trebizond, this being the first occasion in which they have been permitted to touch the army at Eupatoria. They entreat assistance to enable this most necessary movement to be carried out immediately. Every day is of the most urgent consequence.

After it has been effected, they calculate that the force under Selim Pasha will be not less than 25,000 men, composed as follows: 10,000 men at Erzeroom, 6,000 at Trebizond, 8,000 Egyptian, and 3,000 Bashi-Bozouks.

A short time ago the Russians were preparing to evacuate their positions round Kars, but the Seraskier fears they have received information from parties inside. An Armenian had been discovered in the fact of sending an emissary to the enemy with a message to the effect that the garrison had not 14 days' provisions left. The two men had been hanged.

The inhabitants had made an offer to Vassif Pasha to sally out and attack the Russians with 4,000 of the regular troops. This spirited offer had not been immediately accepted, as it was thought better to wait for a combination with Selim Pasha. The distance from Batoom to Kars cannot be effected by a foot passenger in four days. It is 56 hours.

In conclusion, his Excellency turned round to me and said that I was as well aware as he of the continuous exertion made to help the garrison by him, but that from the first we had been agreed on the necessity of a large and well-combined effort. That Omer Pasha had been delayed by causes over which, unfortunately, he could not exercise control. It was an affair of the Alliance. It had all along been understood that such measures as it was in their power to take without the army which had been detained in the Crimea, would not suffice for the object in view: still they had persevered, as in duty bound. His Excellency then proceeded to tell me, with much force, that the Turks were absolutely debarred from executing what was necessary for the prosecution of the campaign, by the delay in giving them the advantage of the Loan.

The grain, to the amount of 1,000,000 kilos, brought by him for the service of the army, was not forwarded to the coast because they could not pay for it.

The Commander of an army at Eupatoria, numbering 35,000 men, had only 300,000 piastres in his chest. When the large reinforcements arrived at Trebizond, there would not be a piastre to buy the animals and supplies needed for their movement.

His Excellency then declared that he had written to the Grand Vizier, that if money were not forthcoming from that source, in a week from this date, he would resign his office.

To this I did not make any reply, but I would earnestly suggest to your Excellency that if means be not taken immediately to supply the military chest of the Turkish Government, it is actually impossible for them to carry on forward movements, or even to keep their troops together.

Perhaps it might be expedient to let them have a sum in advance at once, although the Commissioners may not have terminated their labours; otherwise counsel is unavailing, and the prosecution of the campaign an impossibility. I must entreat your Excellency's pardon for hazarding this suggestion, but I am convinced that in it alone lies the chance of relieving the garrison of Kars, and of ultimate success wherever the Turkish army is concerned.

W. R. MANSFIELD

P.S. I have omitted to mention that his Excellency expressed his belief that the number of Russians in the immediate neighbourhood of Kars does not now exceed 12,000 men.

W. R. M.

Consul Brant to the Earl of Clarendon
(received December 21)

(Extract)   *Erzeroom, November* 27, 1855

I yesterday received a note from General Williams of the 17th, and Major Stuart one of the 21st, both inquiring about Selim Pasha's movements.

The General does not appear to have received any of my notes, and still hopes for relief. Vassif Pasha has also written to Selim Pasha, urging him to make haste. Intelligence has reached Selim Pasha, that 2,000 men had landed at Trebizond, and were hastening on, and on their arrival he promised Major Stuart that he would advance, but pretexts for delay will not be wanting until he will declare it too late. The conduct of Selim Pasha would justify the suspicion that he was sent here expressly to prevent timely succours from reaching Kars and not to press on relief. Such at any rate has been the result of his every action.

It is reported that General Mouravieff has detached some part of his force towards Ahkiska, to strengthen the army which is to oppose Omer Pasha;

if this be confirmed, the retreat of the Kars army may be more easily effected and I hope prove less disastrous than it otherwise would have been, and possibly General Mouravieff may be satisfied with the capture of Kars, and be prudent enough to respect the despair of the army whose valour has already cost him so dear, and thus may leave it unmolested in its retreat.

General Williams desires me to abstain from sending him any letters, as they are sure to fall into the enemy's hands.

Snow fell for the first time at Kars on the 21st instant, but the Russian troops are comfortably hutted, and give no indication of an inclination to retire.

Consul Brant to the Earl of Clarendon
(received December 21)

My Lord,   *Erzeroom, November 27, 1855*
I have the painful duty to announce to your Lordship the surrender of Kars. It was brought this moment by General Kmety.

When General Williams learnt on the 23rd, by a communication from me, that Selim Pasha would not advance, he saw that all hope had vanished. The soldiers were dying by 100 a day of famine. They were mere skeletons and were incapable of fighting or flying. The women brought their children to the General's house for food, and there they left them, and the city was strewed with dead and dying. Under these circumstances the General called together all the Pashas, and asked them if they thought their soldiers could resist longer, or could possibly retreat; they all declared either an impossibility. The next day, General Williams sent Major Teesdale, at 2 P.M. to General Mouravieff's camp, to ask him to appoint an hour the following day for an interview, to treat for a surrender. At sunset, Major Teesdale had not returned, and General Kmety and General Kolman left with a guard of Koords to cut their way through the Russian patrols. They passed several and at last were stopped by one, and separated, and it was after 24 hours that they rejoined each other, and in three days and nights they reached this in safety. General Kmety does not know more than above stated as to terms, but he says the garrison being in so distressed a state, it must submit to any conditions General Mouravieff chose to dictate.

I am hurried to save [catch] the post, but tomorrow will send off an express messenger with such further particulars as I can learn.

JAMES BRANT

Consul Brant to the Earl of Clarendon
(received December 27)

(Extract) *Erzeroom, November* 28, 1855

I had the honour yesterday evening to address your Lordship a few hasty lines, to inform you that Kars had offered to capitulate.

General Kmety had then just arrived from thence, having, with General Kolman, escaped the Russian patrols. He was charged by Brigadier-General Sir William Williams to communicate to me

the fall of Kars, and the sad events which preceded it.
Late on the 22nd a foot messenger reached him with
a packet from me. This was the first he had received
since that which conveyed the news of the fall of
Sebastopol, several weeks before. The General kept its
contents secret for 24 hours. He then called in from
his out-stations General Kmety, and told him how little hope my communication held out of assistance
from Selim Pasha; and seeing that famine, which had
already filled the hospitals with sick, was beginning to
produce a serious mortality among the troops—about
80 having died that day—and their bread being
reduced to a few days, he declared he could see no
possibility of holding out any longer, and he proposed
next morning assembling the Pashas, to consider their
position. Early on the morning of the 24th all the
Pashas assembled, and their actual situation, with their
prospects, was clearly laid before them by the
General, who asked them whether a prolonged
defence was possible, or whether the troops could or
would attempt a retreat. Both questions were
answered in the negative by every Pasha declaring the
men, with few exceptions, were not in a physical or
moral condition to march or fight. The General then
proposed that he should request an interview of
General Mouravieff for the next day, to treat for
terms, which being thankfully acceded to, at about
half-past 2 P.M. of the 24th, Major Teesdale was dispatched with the message to the Russian camp.

When the decision to retreat was adopted,
Generals Kmety and Kolman requested General

Williams to accept their resignation, and to allow them to make their way through the Russian patrols. They had been condemned to death by the Austrian Government, for the part they had taken in the Hungarian War of Independence, and they expected that, if made prisoners they should be delivered up by the Russians to their Government, and their fate would be in such case certain. General Williams promised to do all in his power to make special conditions for them, but as their swords had now become useless, they entreated permission to retire, to which the General consented, after thanking them in the warmest and most feeling terms for their gallantry and good service.

Major Teesdale had not returned by nightfall from the Russian camp, and Generals Kmety and Kolman, wishing to profit of an hour of darkness before the rising of the moon, to glide by the Russian patrols unmolested, took their leave of their companions in arms, and accompanied by five brave and trusty Koords, hired as an escort, quitted the famine-stricken city. The party by their knowledge of the modes of challenging the Russian patrols, passed close by two unmolested, but a third recognised them, and they were obliged to disperse over the hills, and met again 24 hours afterwards at a place of rendezvous fixed on, and from thence they came hither without further rencontre, after riding uninterruptedly for three days and nights. General Kmety says that the position of the garrison and city was such that any conditions, however hard, must be accepted. Human nature could neither resist longer nor endure more. Scarcely 1,000 men of the whole garrison were in a state to use their weapons, and not many more could have sustained a march pursued by an enemy. Had a retreat been attempted very few would have survived it; those who escaped the arms of the enemy would have died of exhaustion. The women crowded round the General's house with their starving children crying for food, and throwing down their little ones at his gate, would not depart but with food. Himself, whom it had been their delight to salute and recognise as he passed they no longer noticed kindly, but hurried by with an ominous half-averted scowl; the same look was perceived in the soldiers; and how must this have lacerated a breast which always overflowed with tenderness towards suffering humanity.

Lieutenant-Colonel Lake was suffering from gout, brought on by night patrolling and fatigue in the trenches; Mr Zohrab was laid up with typhus, but was recovering; the other officers were well. Nothing is yet known as to the conditions of the surrender; probably a few days will inform us.

General Kmety says that Sir William Williams had received the information of the honour conferred on him by Her Majesty, and that when he congratulated him, Sir William thanked him in a few words and with a faint smile; his mind was then overwhelmed by painful feelings, and occupied by the impending calamity, and he could scarce feel pleasure even at the honour received.

*Brigadier-General Williams to the Earl of Clarendon
(received January 6, 1856)*

*Russian Camp near Kars,
November 29, 1855*

My Lord,

From the various despatches in cypher which I have addressed to your Lordship through Mr Brant, the intelligence which I have now the misfortune to announce must have been expected by your Lordship.

I had received direct promises of succour from Selim Pasha; and Omer Pasha's operations, until I knew that his movements were directed towards Soukoum-Kaleh, had buoyed me up in my determination to hold out to the last moment; this intelligence from the Generalissimo reached me on the 24th instant, by the same post which brought me positive news, from Mr Brant, of the indisposition or inability of Selim Pasha to advance further than Kupri-Keuy.

We had, up to that date, suffered from cold, want of sufficient clothing, and starvation, without a murmur escaping from the troops. They fell dead at their posts, in their tents, and throughout the camp, as brave men should who cling to their duty through the slightest glimmering of hope of saving a place entrusted to their custody. From the day of their glorious victory, on the 29th September, they had not tasted animal food, and their nourishment consisted of two-fifths of a ration of bread and the roots of grass, which they had scarcely strength to dig for; yet night and day they stood to their arms, their wasted frames showing the fearful effects of starvation, but their sparkling eyes telling me what they would do were the enemy again to attack them.

We had now lost nearly 2,000 men by starvation, and the townspeople also suffered, and would have died by hundreds if I had not divided the bread of the soldiers amongst those who had bravely fought by their side. I therefore begged the Mushir to call a council of war, which, on being told that we had only six days' rations, came unanimously to the conclusion that nothing was left to us but a capitulation; and that the debility of the men, and total want of Cavalry, Field Artillery, and ammunition mules, rendered any attempt to retreat impossible.

The Mushir then deputed me to treat with General Mouravieff, and I consequently waited on his Excellency on the 25th instant. He at first seemed determined to make prisoners of all who defended the place, but as the Redif, or Militia, and the townspeople formed a large portion of the Infantry, I made a successful appeal to his humanity, which, coupled with the obvious measure of destroying our artillery and stores, to which we should have had recourse previous to an unconditional surrender, brought about the Convention which I have now the honour to enclose for your Lordship's information, without the expression of unavailing regret.

I have only to add that the stipulations were carried into effect yesterday; that myself, my officers, and the regular troops composing the last garrison, amounting to 8,000 of all arms, are prisoners of war, and that the Irregulars, numbering 6,000, have marched towards their respective homes.

I and my officers are to march for Tiflis tomorrow, there to await the decision of the Emperor as to the place of our abode in Russia.

W. F. WILLIAMS

Enclosure

Précis of the Convention between General Mouravieff and Major-General Sir William Williams, relative to the surrender of Kars

1. The fortress of Kars shall be delivered up intact.
2. The garrison of Kars, with the Turkish Commander-in-chief, shall march out with the honours of war, and become prisoners. The officers, in consideration of their gallant defence of the place, shall retain their swords.
3. The private property of the whole garrison shall be respected.
4. The Redifs (militia), Bashi-Bozouks and Laz, shall be allowed to return to their homes.
5. The non-combatants, such as medical officers, scribes, and hospital attendants, shall be allowed to return to their homes.
6. General Williams shall be allowed the privilege of making a list of certain Hungarian and other European officers, to enable them to return to their homes.

7. The persons mentioned in Articles 4, 5, and 6, are in honour bound not to serve against Russia during the present war.
8. The inhabitants of Kars will be protected, in their persons and property.
9. The public buildings and the monuments of the town will be respected.

November 27, 1855

DECEMBER 1855

General Williams to the Earl of Clarendon
(received January, 1856)

(Extract)   *Gumri, December* 2, 1855

I have arrived thus far on my long journey, receiving, at every step, the kindest offices of, I may say, every officer in the Russian army, from the highest to the lowest.

Lord Stratford de Redcliffe to the Earl of Clarendon
(received December 14)

(Extract)   *Therapia, December* 3, 1855

Intelligence from Kars, of necessity brief and secret, continues to augur ill for the fate of the gallant army beleaguered in that fortress. The latest accounts are from Mr Brant, who has sent them on to your Lordship. His despatch of the 20th ultimo reached me the night before last, and I lost not an instant in sending instructions to General Mansfield and M. Pisani. At this late hour nothing can possibly be attempted otherwise than in the spirit of a forlorn hope, but I am anxious that no stone should be left unturned on our side that may afford a chance of relief. I have been careful to bring the conduct of Selim Pasha under the notice of the Porte, and especially under that of his responsible chief, the Seraskier; suggesting at the same time the advantage which might be derived from sending a British officer, if not to take the command of the Turkish forces at Erzeroom, at least to advise with some degree of authority.

Enclosed herewith in copy is General Mansfield's report of his discussion with the Seraskier. I have nothing to add, except that Admiral Grey affords at my request all the assistance in his power for the transport of Turkish troops to Trebizond.

Enclosure

Brigadier-General Mansfield to Lord Stratford de Redcliffe
(Extract)   *Pera, December 2,* 1855

I have the honour to return Mr Brant's despatch, and to inform your Excellency that, in company with M. Etienne Pisani, I this morning visited the Seraskier Pasha. A conversation ensued in accordance with your Excellency's instructions.

His Excellency observed that by this time three out of four battalions of Infantry, sent from hence to reinforce Selim Pasha at Erzeroom, must have arrived. He is, consequently, now at the head of about 13,500 men. After the Council sat, of which your Excellency was informed in my despatch of the 25th ultimo, an order was sent to Selim Pasha in the name of the Sultan, to run all hazards for the relief of Kars. That order will reach him tomorrow. Till the arrival of the reinforcement above alluded to, Selim Pasha was deterred from moving, on account of the presence of a moveable Russian corps of observation on the Byazid road, consisting of from 5,000 to 6,000 men. The Pasha could not, with regard to that corps, leave Erzeroom altogether without troops.

His Excellency did not understand why the garrison of Kars did not attempt a sortie.

Mr Brant was in error in supposing Selim Pasha would not obey Vassif Pasha, on account of the former being the senior in rank. The reverse is the case; besides that, Vassif Pasha has been nominated Commander-in-chief of all the troops in the country where the operations are going on. Selim Pasha is a brave energetic man, and possessed of much experience. He commanded a division in the Egyptian campaign, when Sir Charles Napier was successful, and has been in several general actions. He is not a man who has been educated in a school, but his practical knowledge is considerable; the Seraskier is in the act of sending to his assistance on his staff, Mouhlip Pasha, alias Stourdja, of Wallachia, who distinguished himself much on the Danube and is highly educated.

Three steamers, two British and one Turkish, have gone to Eupatoria to ship Egyptians for Trebizond. As soon as Admiral Grey reported another to be ready, which his Excellency expected immediately, it would proceed on the same day.

In conclusion, his Excellency assured me that the minutes of the last Council had been sent to Selim Pasha, with an injunction to spare no exertion, and that he could not be held responsible if his army were lost in the attempt to help the garrison of Kars.

Major Stuart to the Earl of Clarendon
(received January 1, 1856)

(Extract)   *Erzeroom, December 5, 1855*

Referring to my letter of the 28th ultimo, I have the honour to inform you that intelligence has since been received which confirms the fact of the surrender of Kars.

The latest accounts from that place are to the 27th ultimo, on which day the terms of capitulation were signed; on the 28th the Russians were to march in; and General Williams, Colonel Lake, Major Teesdale, and Captain Thompson, were to proceed under escort to Tiflis.

Mr Churchill, Secretary to General Williams, was, at his own request, permitted to accompany him.

It would appear that General Mouravieff evinced on this occasion all the consideration that was due to the brave garrison with which he had to deal; with the exception of General Williams and the Mushir, all the officers were allowed to retain their swords. The non-combatants were not included among prisoners. The Redif troops, numbering about 9,000, were dismissed to their homes; but the Nizam, between 4,000 and 5,000 strong, were to be sent to Georgia.

A special stipulation was also agreed to, that liberty should be granted to such persons as General Williams should think fit to name. The General peremptorily insisted upon this point, his object being to provide for the safety of those European officers in the Turkish army who were serving with him: among those who received the benefit of it was Baron Schwartzenburg; he arrived here on the 3rd instant, and from him I have obtained the foregoing particulars. He also mentioned that the last ration was drawn from the stores before he left; but immediately after the capitulation was signed, 200 horses laden with provisions were sent by Mouravieff into the town.

I have not yet heard from General Williams; but he sent word to say he would write from Gumri.

The Earl of Clarendon to Lord Stratford de Redcliffe

My Lord,   *Foreign Office, December* 7, 1855

I have received your Excellency's despatch of the 26th of November, and I have to inform you in reply that Her Majesty's Government entirely approve the steps which you have taken with a view to the relief of Kars.

CLARENDON

Lord Stratford de Redcliffe to the Earl of Clarendon
(received December 9)

(Telegraph)   *Therapia, December* 8, 1855, 1.30 A.M.

I learn with the deepest concern by despatches of the 27th November, just received from Her Majesty's Consul at Erzeroom, that Vassif Pasha and General Williams have been reduced by a painful necessity to despair of saving Kars from the enemy. Mr Brant has not stated, nor indeed does he appear to have known, what conditions, if any, had been settled.

Major Teesdale had been sent on the 23rd to propose an interview with General Mouravieff for the purpose of treating for a surrender. That officer not having returned at sunset, General Kmety and General Kolman were sent to force their way through the Russian patrols, and finally in three days reached Erzeroom, where Selim Pasha was thought to have been remiss in not attempting the relief of the besieged fortress.

Lord Stratford de Redcliffe to the Earl of Clarendon
(received December 21)

(Extract)   *Therapia, December* 10, 1855

Enclosed in copy is a report of General Mansfield's conversation with the Seraskier Pasha, when he waited upon that Minister at my request after the arrival of the last despatches from Erzeroom.

Enclosure

Brigadier-General Mansfield to Lord Stratford de Redcliffe
(Extract)   *Pera, December* 8, 1855

Not having thought it advisable to defer making your Excellency's important communication to the Seraskier, in the absence of M. Pisani, I took the liberty of soliciting Mr Doria to accompany me to his Excellency, to which he willingly acceded.

I communicated the substance of the deplorable accounts from Erzeroom, and dwelt very urgently upon the reports of Mr Brant, on the conduct of Selim Pasha. His Excellency showed me the despatches of Selim Pasha, as well as the original ones of Vassif Pasha. The despatch of Selim Pasha, giving the account of the surrender, was not in the packet which had arrived from Erzeroom, although there was one from the Civil Governor alluding to it, and confirmatory of the account of the Consul.

In respect of the accusations preferred against Selim, it must be said that there has been no attempt at concealment on his part. The despatches of Vassif were laid before me, in which the former was strongly

urged to come to the assistance of Kars, while attention was directed to the Russian moveable column on
the side of Byazid.

Arrangements have been made by Selim for the
collection of provisions at Olti and Penek, and the
Kaimakam of Childir had, by his orders, collected 5,000
horses with arabas to convey them into Kars, if the vigilance of the enemy relaxed in any degree. I urged his
Excellency to consider well the present position of
Selim Pasha. Assuming that Vassif Pasha is in the hands
of the enemy, on the Commander at Erzeroom now
devolved the task of defending the country altogether.
The relief of Kars was a single operation. The sphere of
his duty would now be very largely extended.

He seemed to feel what I advanced, but said
there must be inquiry to ascertain if he failed from
want of forethought and energy, or whether he had
been prudent in not risking incomplete action with
imperfect means, which, while endangering his
force, could produce no real result. He must have
time to consider the question, prior to laying his
views before the Council, which would assemble to
consider the subject.

His Excellency was perfectly frank, and much
time was spent in reading every despatch in the hopes
of additional light being thrown on the matter. He
repeated more than once that when they had sent
Selim Pasha to Kars, their object was to send their
best man.

When I expressed your Excellency's assurance
that Her Majesty's Government would be much hurt

if no effort had been made to save the fortress, his answer was: "And what must our Government feel?" The last advices from Omer Pasha himself are unimportant. But the messenger who brought the latest account said that the advanced guard of the army under his Highness was within four hours of Kutais, and the main body within six hours. According to him, Omer Pasha had signified to the Commanders that the advance was to be made immediately. Batoom had now become the base of operation. A large quantity of provisions had been thrown into Redoute-Kaleh. The road to that place was quite open from the camp of Omer Pasha. Mustafa Pasha was still near Ozurgheti, having been ordered by Omer Pasha not to advance till his Highness had crossed the Rhion.

Various advices go to show that the strength of the Russians before Kars is considerably under 20,000 men. Letters from one Arslan Bey in the fortress, which I saw, give details of a Russian division having left the army before Kars and gone to Ahkiska in consequence of the march of Omer Pasha. In like manner it is believed that the Cossacks who have been so long at Ardahan, blocking the road from Kars to Batoom, have gone to Akhalkhileh in two divisions. But this report having come from Kars, which is twelve hours' distance from Ardahan, perfect reliance cannot be placed on it.

When my very lengthened visit was brought to a close, the hour was too late for me to visit Fuad Pasha. But the Seraskier assured me that he would bring your Excellency's communication most seriously before the Council; and while I was with his Excellency, the despatches which had arrived from Erzeroom during my visit, were sent to the private residence of the Minister for Foreign Affairs.

Lord Stratford de Redcliffe to the Earl of Clarendon *(received December 27)*

My Lord,   *Constantinople, December* 14, 1855
We are still without intelligence of the actual surrender of Kars and its garrison into the hands of the enemy, but no doubt of the fact appears to have been entertained at Erzeroom, when the last dispatches under date of the 29th ultimo, came away.

Though sealed reports, which may be presumed to contain the same statements as those addressed to me, are forwarded by the present occasion to your Lordship, yet, as I have no certain knowledge of their contents, I forward herewith copies of the despatches which I have myself received from Mr Brant and Major Stuart.

Your Lordship will observe that the number of men under arms in the fortress, which I fear is in Russian hands at this moment, is stated by the latter at 15,000 men, and the fall of the place from famine is the more to be deplored as the works appear to have been well provided with means of defence in other respects. Seventy pieces of field artillery, in addition to the guns in position, form a severe item of loss.

I have made a full communication of the painful correspondence to Fuad Pasha and his principal colleagues. M. Pisani informs me that they listened to it in silence. The conduct of Selim Pasha, as characterised by Mr Brant and Major Stuart, ought to produce his recall and consignment to a court-martial. I am not yet acquainted with the Porte's intentions.

STRATFORD DE REDCLIFFE

Enclosure 1

Consul Brant to Lord Stratford de Redcliffe
(Extract)   *Erzeroom, November* 28, 1855
I have the honour to inform your Excellency that the garrison of Kars contained, at the moment it was about to surrender, about 20,000 men receiving rations, out of which there was not above 10,000 combatants, 66 siege guns, with 70 beautiful pieces of field artillery, and 500 rounds per gun. There were about 2,000 good Minié rifles, and the muskets of the troops, with about 340,000 rounds of ball cartridge. Everything else had been used up.

This loss may be attributed to the dilatory proceedings of Omer Pasha, who about two months ago promised to relieve the Kars garrison, and to the cowardice of Selim Pasha, who, had he been courageous enough to have advanced, might have enabled the garrison to have made an effective sortie, or at least to have effected an honourable retreat.

There are now, and have been for months past, in this city, about 20 Pashas I believe, who literally may be said to do nothing but receive their extravagant appointments, and ruin the country by their exactions.

Enclosure 2

Major Stuart to Lord Stratford de Redcliffe

My Lord,   *Erzeroom, November* 28, 1855

I have the honour to inform you that yesterday afternoon General Kmety arrived here unexpectedly from Kars, with intelligence that leaves but little doubt that that place with its garrison, including General Williams and his immediate staff, and all the munitions of war it contained, are now in the hands of the Russians.

The circumstances communicated by General Kmety are as follows:

On the 23rd instant General Williams received a letter informing him that no succour would be sent to him by Selim Pasha, the Mushir in command here. On the morning of the 24th, he called together all the general officers holding commands in Kars, explained to them the position in which they stood, that there were but six days' provisions remaining in store, that matters were approaching to an extremity, and put it to them severally, if their troops were in a condition to attempt to cut their way through the Russian lines. The answer of all was to the effect that such an attempt would be utterly impossible, owing to the state of the men, debilitated as they were by long continued severe work and insufficient food. This being the case no alternative remained but capitulation, and accordingly at 2 or 3 P.M. of the 24th, Major Teesdale was sent to Mouravieff, to request he would appoint an hour for the settlement of terms. Major Teesdale had not returned at sunset, when General Kmety, in company with General Kolman, left Kars, with a few Koords as guides to make their escape; they succeeded with difficulty in getting through the lines, and riding day and night got in here, as I said, yesterday. I should observe that these officers being Hungarian refugees, were afraid of surrendering to the Russians, lest they should be handed over to the Austrian Government, and it was with General Williams' entire consent that they left Kars in the above manner.

The condition of Kars as described by General Kmety must have been deplorable. The hospitals were crowded; 70 or 80 men a day were dying of exhaustion, and all were reduced to an extreme degree of debility and emaciation: add to this that desertions in large numbers were of constant occurrence. With respect to the inhabitants of the place, their case was, if possible, worse; they had nothing but what was sparingly given them from the military stores, and General Williams had every day to endure the sight of women bringing their children to his door and leaving them there to die.

The garrison numbered, as nearly as I could learn, about 15,000; there were 70 field guns, 66 garrison guns, with 500 rounds of ammunition, and about 20,000 stand of small arms, including 2,000 excellent Miniés. I again affirm that this loss might have been averted had there been in command here a man of courage and ability. The number of troops at hand were sufficient for the purpose, but I greatly fear that Selim Pasha is altogether wanting in those military qualities which such an occasion called for.

ROBERT STUART

Lord Stratford de Redcliffe to the Earl of Clarendon
(received December 30)

My Lord,   *Constantinople, December* 14, 1855
I learn from M. de Thouvenel that permission has at length arrived from Paris for Marshal Pélissier to assent to the departure of the Egyptian Infantry at Eupatoria for Trebizond. I am informed, however, that the Turkish Commander had declared his determination to embark the troops without waiting for any further communication; and it is certain that English vessels, exposed by the delay to much tempestuous weather, were ready to receive them on board. If it be true, as stated on the alleged authority of the French Commander-in-chief, that out of the 10,000 Egyptians, 6,000 are affected by scurvy, I fear that little will be gained by the transfer of the healthy portion of them to Trebizond.

I avail myself of this opportunity to forward in copy for your Lordship's information the correspondence which has passed on this subject between Sir William Codrington and myself. I add the copy of a report from Her Majesty's Acting Vice-Consul at

Trebizond, where a small reinforcement of about 800 Infantry had arrived.

STRATFORD DE REDCLIFFE

Enclosure 1

General Sir W. Codrington to Lord Stratford de Redcliffe
Headquarters near Sebastopol,
(Extract) *December 10, 1855*
I wrote to Marshal Pélissier in the general tone of your letter, expressing to him the great object it seemed to be to get the Turkish troops to Trebizond, and that, if done at all, it should be done at once, and offering my assistance, if I could, by communications with our navy, further this object.

His answer was, that he could not consent to their leaving Eupatoria without the express sanction of the Emperor of the French.

Enclosure 2

Lord Stratford de Redcliffe to General Sir W. Codrington
(Extract) *Constantinople, December 12,* 1855
The Turks are sadly mortified by the embargo which appears to have been laid on the Egyptian troops at Eupatoria.

Supposing the surrender of Kars to be confirmed, the Turks, I imagine, will still be anxious to send reinforcements to Erzeroom with all practicable speed, notwithstanding the lateness of the season.

Enclosure 3

Acting Consul Stevens to Lord Stratford de Redcliffe

My Lord,   *Trebizond, December 3, 1855*

I have the honour to inform your Lordship that 850 Turkish troops landed here yesterday from the steamer "Stella," which vessel arrived the day before yesterday from Constantinople. I regret to state that the cholera manifested itself among these men; two fatal cases occurred on board, and two more since they landed, and there are 14 under treatment in Dr Farquhar's hospital.

G. A. STEVENS

General Williams to the Earl of Clarendon
(received January, 1856)

(Extract)   *Tiflis, December 14, 1855*

I send these few lines, through General Mouravieff, to apprise your Lordship of the arrival of myself and Staff in this city. We were conveyed in carriages furnished by the Russian Government, and under the charge of Captain Baschmakoff, of the Imperial Guard, whose kind and friendly care of us demands our best thanks; indeed, nothing can exceed the warm and flattering reception which we have received from the authorities, military and civil.

We may, in ten days, hear the Emperor's decision as to the place of our abode during the time we shall remain prisoners of war; but, I believe, little doubt is felt by General Mouravieff that Moscow will be the point upon which we shall march.

The Earl of Clarendon to Lord Stratford de Redcliffe

My Lord,   *Foreign Office, December* 15, 1855

I have to state to your Excellency that Her Majesty's Government approve of the steps taken by you with reference to the precarious state of affairs at Kars, as reported in your despatch of the 3rd instant.

CLARENDON

Lord Stratford de Redcliffe to the Earl of Clarendon
(received December 30)

My Lord,   *Constantinople, December* 17, 1855

Though I have nothing myself from Erzeroom of a later date than the end of November, I have seen a letter, copy enclosed, from Trebizond, which leaves no doubt that the fortress of Kars and its garrison had fallen into the hands of the Russians. It is a consolation to find that the conditions may fairly be termed honourable under such disastrous circumstances as we must conclude to have existed from the previous accounts.

The Porte has received intelligence similar in substance to what is stated in the letter from Trebizond.

STRATFORD DE REDCLIFFE

Enclosure

Extract from a letter from Trebizond, dated
December 11, 1855

No authentic accounts had reached Erzeroom on
the 4th of December, of the surrender of Kars, but
it was known that the terms obtained by General
Williams were most honourable. All the officers
retained their swords in consequence of their heroic
conduct on the 29th September. Redif and Bashi-
Bozouks, all civil people and non-combatants, all
Nogars, and 25 people to be named by General
Williams, without any inquiry into reason, set at
liberty. Dr Sandwith, Keane, and Rennisson, and
Zohrab, the interpreter, were hourly expected at
Erzeroom. Mr Churchill having fought in command of a battery on the 29th September,
detained, and will be sent to Tiflis with General
Williams. Some of the Nogars had reached
Erzeroom; they left the evening before the
Russians were to take possession. Omer Pasha is at
a standstill in consequence of the heavy rains and
swamps; he was on the Sieva, in tents, on the 30th
of November.

Lord Stratford de Redcliffe to the Earl of Clarendon
(received December 30)

My Lord,   *Constantinople, December* 18, 1855
I have the honour to transmit to your Lordship herewith, the copy of a despatch from Mr Consul Brant,
dated the 3rd instant, stating the conditions of the

capitulation of Kars as reported by some Hungarian officers recently arrived at Erzeroom.

STRATFORD DE REDCLIFFE

Enclosure

Consul Brant to Lord Stratford de Redcliffe

My Lord,   *Erzeroom, December* 3, 1855

I have the honour to inform your Excellency that yesterday some Hungarian officers arrived, and the conditions of the capitulation were learned from their report. They were sent off in haste to be out of the way before the Russian army entered the city, and Sir William Williams could not therefore write, but I am in momentary expectation of receiving a letter from him.

On the 24th at nightfall, Generals Kmety and Kolman left Kars. It was some time afterwards that Major Teesdale returned from the Russian camp; he was retained to dine, and was treated with most marked politeness. On the 25th General Williams had his interview with General Mouravieff, which passed off satisfactorily. On the 26th Ekrem Effendi, first Secretary of the Mushir, Vassif Pasha, went to the Russian camp to make some arrangement, and on the 27th, Hafiz Pasha went. On that evening, the Hungarian officers left under a Russian guard, and they received everything necessary while thus escorted.

The conditions of the surrender are stated to be, that all non-combatants should be allowed to depart, as also all foreigners in the Turkish service whose countries are not at war with Russia. Also the Turkish Redif, with their officers, and the Bashi-Bozouks; private property is to be respected; all the British and Turkish officers, and regular troops are to remain prisoners of war; all the arms, guns, and ammunition to be surrendered, but the officers, in consequence of their heroic defence of the 29th of September, are allowed to retain their swords.

Thus far, if the report be true, the capitulation seems to be as favourable to the party surrendering as generous on the part of the victors, and I feel convinced these conditions are mainly attributable to the tact and noble bearing of General Williams. To the General and his Staff, General Mouravieff and his officers were most courteous, and it would appear that, for so heavy a calamity, everything was conducted in a manner creditable and satisfactory to both parties.

A Colonel, whose name I could not learn, was particularly attentive and communicative; he said it was a great fault for Omer Pasha to have invaded Georgia from the coast, and they had little apprehension of his successes on that side, and his army would probably be lost in the forests and marshes if it did not make a timely retreat, but if Omer Pasha had come by Erzeroom, things would have been changed.

Dr Sandwith will quit Kars when he has put in order and delivered over the hospitals.

Mr Zohrab was as yet too weak to be removed after his severe attack of typhus; Mr Rennisson will come with them. Mr Churchill, though free to retire, it is said will remain with General Williams. I will not attempt to give other details on mere hearsay, when, probably, everything will be soon reported in an authentic shape.

JAS. BRANT

The Earl of Clarendon to Lord Cowley

(Extract)   *Foreign Office, December* 19, 1855

I transmit to your Excellency herewith a copy of a despatch [dated November 19, 1855] from Lieutenant-Colonel Simmons.

Your Excellency will communicate this despatch to the French Government, and point out the danger to which the army of Omer Pasha is now exposed, and the urgent necessity for the formation of an army of reserve.

The Emperor and Marshal Vaillant have long been aware of the great importance attached by Her Majesty's Government to the relief of Kars, and the disastrous news which has recently arrived proves that their apprehensions as to its probable fate were but too well founded. But if prompt and decisive measures are not taken, the fall of Kars will be followed by the worst consequences. Masters of that strong fortress, threatening Erzeroom, and commanding all the mountain passes, the Russians may be able to force the whole of Koordistan and the Armenian population to assist them against the Sultan; and the allies may in a few months learn that far greater danger threatens the Ottoman Empire from the side of Asia than from Europe. In fact, the object of the war will be defeated if the integrity of that Empire is not secured from attack on every side, and at all events the military operations for next year must to a certain extent depend upon whether Asia Minor is placed in a position of adequate defence.

At the present moment and until the necessary measures are deliberated and determined upon, Her Majesty's Government have to suggest that the Turkish forces now at Eupatoria should, without delay, be conveyed to Trebizond, and placed under the command of Omer Pasha for the purpose of forming an army of reserve applicable either to the defence of Erzeroom or to serve as a reinforcement to the army now with Omer Pasha in Mingrelia.

The Earl of Clarendon to Major-General Williams
Sir,   *Foreign Office, December* 22, 1855
Her Majesty's Government have learned with the deepest regret that the garrison of Kars was reduced by famine to capitulate, and that in consequence yourself and the other British officers serving under you at that place have fallen as prisoners of war into the hands of the Russians.

Her Majesty's Government have observed with the utmost admiration the zealous and indefatigable exertions which you made for the defence of that important position under circumstances of no ordinary difficulty, as well as the judgment and energy which you displayed in overcoming the obstacles of every sort with which you had to contend, and in inspiring the Turkish soldiery with that confidence which enabled them, under your influence, signally to defeat on all occasions the attempts made by an enemy superior in numbers and military resources to make themselves masters by force of arms of the besieged town.

I trust that the applications which have been made to the Russian Government for your exchange may be successful, and that Her Majesty will soon again have at her disposal the services of an officer who has earned for himself so distinguished a reputation. Some time may elapse before you receive this despatch, but I think it right at once to place on record the sentiments of Her Majesty and of her Government in regard to your whole conduct during the time that you have been employed with the Turkish army in Asia; and, while sympathising with you in the unfortunate result of your honourable exertions, I have to express Her Majesty's entire approval of the manner in which you acquitted yourself throughout the whole period of your recent services.

I have at the same time to instruct you to signify to the officers and civilians serving under your orders at Kars, namely, to Colonel Lake, to Major Teesdale, to Captain Thompson, to Mr Churchill, and to Dr Sandwith, Her Majesty's entire approval of their conduct.

CLARENDON

Lord Cowley to the Earl of Clarendon
(received December 24)

(Extract)   *Paris, December* 22, 1855

In compliance with the instructions contained in your Lordship's despatch of the 19th instant, which only reached me late at night on the 20th, I saw Marshal Vaillant this afternoon on the subject of permitting the Ottoman troops now at Eupatoria to proceed at once to Asia Minor.

The Marshal said that as far back as the 12th instant the French Government had consented to the departure of the Egyptian Division for Trebizond, and intelligence had been immediately sent by telegraph to Marshal Pélissier. On the other hand his Excellency had learnt by a telegraphic despatch of the 16th instant from the Crimea, which had crossed his of the 12th on the road, that the Egyptian Division must have left Eupatoria about that time.

To a further request made by me, in furtherance of your Lordship's instructions, to Marshal Vaillant, that the whole of the Turkish force now at Eupatoria should be set free and replaced by a part of the troops now before Sebastopol, his Excellency replied that he had no objection, if it were practicable.

The Earl of Clarendon to Lord Stratford de Redcliffe

My Lord,   *Foreign Office, December* 28, 1855

I need scarcely state to your Excellency that the news of the capitulation of Kars was received by Her Majesty's Government with the deepest pain and regret, and with a feeling of bitter disappointment that no attempt was made by Selim Pasha to save that place from the enemy.

It appears from the despatches of Her Majesty's Consul at Erzeroom, which have passed through your hands, that Selim Pasha was in command of a force which, under an active general officer, was capable of relieving Kars, but that he had shown no capacity or energy, and had evinced nothing but a steady repugnance to make any movements to rescue the brave garrison which was compelled at last to surrender to the Russian General, Mouravieff.

Mr Brant accuses Selim Pasha of incapacity, and even cowardice, and states, that although repeatedly urged in the strongest terms by Major Stuart, the senior British officer at Erzeroom, to advance and relieve Kars, he had returned a refusal to every entreaty addressed to him.

Her Majesty's Government, who are making such vast efforts and sacrifices to uphold the Ottoman Empire, are entitled to demand that a signal example should be made of an officer who has conducted himself as Selim Pasha is said to have done, and I have accordingly to instruct your Excellency to call upon the Porte to order an immediate and searching investigation into this case, and if the charges brought against Selim Pasha should prove to be well founded, to visit that officer with heavy punishment and disgrace.

CLARENDON

The Earl of Clarendon to Lord Stratford de Redcliffe

My Lord,   *Foreign Office, December* 31, 1855

I have to instruct your Excellency to make known to the Porte that, in the opinion of Her Majesty's Government, it is of urgent importance that reinforcements should be sent from Constantinople to Trebizond to go on to Erzeroom. Her Majesty's Government hope that the Turkish fleet, which has now nothing to do, may be employed on this service.

CLARENDON

Lord Stratford de Redcliffe to the Earl of Clarendon
(received January 20, 1856)

My Lord,   *Constantinople, December* 31, 1855

With reference to my other despatch of this date, I have the honour to transmit herewith another despatch which I addressed to Her Majesty's Consul at Erzeroom, acquainting him with the Porte's intention to supersede the Mushir of Erzeroom by Vedgihi Pasha, formerly Governor of Saida.

STRATFORD DE REDCLIFFE

Enclosure

Lord Stratford de Redcliffe to Consul Brant

(Extract)   *Constantinople, December* 30, 1855

It will be agreeable to you to know that I have succeeded in obtaining from the Porte a promise that the two respective Mushirs of Erzeroom and of the army, Mehemet and Selim Pashas, shall be forthwith superseded.

The present intention, as announced to me from the Porte, is that Vedgihi Pasha, formerly at Saida, shall replace the former, and Ismail Pasha, who is now here from the Danube, the latter.

It is possible, however, that Omer Pasha, who has retired on Redoute-Kaleh, may take the command in person.

I have to request that you will consider this communication of the Porte's intentions as intended for the present for your own information alone.

P.S. The Porte has made me acquainted with its intention to send 10,000 men of Omer Pasha's army to Erzeroom.

I fear that the Egyptian troops landed from Eupatoria at Trebizond by means of transports furnished by Her Majesty's Naval Commanders, will suffer greatly from the fatigue of their march over such mountainous roads, and in an impaired state of health.

Lord Stratford de Redcliffe to the Earl of Clarendon
(received January 20, 1856)

(Extract)   *Constantinople, December* 31, 1855

Selim Pasha, who has obtained so unhappy a distinction at Erzeroom, was recommended to his command there by Fethi Ahmed Pasha, the Master of the Ordnance. The Seraskier, who is now in office, made the official appointment under a persuasion, he declares, that he was qualified to render good service in the field. I understood when the appointment was communicated to me, that Selim Pasha was only invested with the command of the reinforcements destined for Erzeroom.

General Mansfield informs me that General Guyon, in speaking of Selim Pasha, described him as a man of undoubted courage; and I have heard the same character of him from another British officer. It appears that his intelligence is not rated so high as his bravery: and your Lordship is well aware how difficult it is to find among the candidates for high military employment in Turkey individuals distinguished for capacity and professional knowledge.

JANUARY 1856

Consul Brant to the Earl of Clarendon
(received January, 1856)

(Extract)   *Erzeroom, January* 3, 1856

I have the honour to acknowledge your Lordship's despatch of the 10th of December, approving of the steps I took in endeavouring to persuade Selim Pasha to march to the relief of Kars. I only regret that all the endeavours of Major Stuart and myself failed; for, as your Lordship will have perceived by a subsequent despatch, had the Mushir advanced, General Mouravieff would probably have retreated, and Kars have been saved without even a battle.

The Earl of Clarendon to Lord Stratford de Redcliffe
(Extract)   *Foreign Office, January* 10, 1856
The Porte can neither hope for the success of the Sultan's arms, nor for the co-operation of his allies, if signal examples are not made of men like Selim and Tahir Pashas, of whose cowardice and treachery there now exist such overwhelming proofs.

Lord Stratford de Redcliffe to the Earl of Clarendon
(received January 29)
My Lord,   *Constantinople, January* 14, 1856
I communicated to Fuad Pasha your Lordship's instruction requiring the trial and, eventually, the punishment of Selim Pasha. His Excellency's answer, after communicating with his colleagues, may be expressed in the following words: a searching inquiry into the conduct of Selim Pasha is already ordered by the Porte, and should the charges brought against him prove to be well grounded, he will be punished accordingly.

STRATFORD DE REDCLIFFE

Lord Stratford de Redcliffe to the Earl of Clarendon
(received January 29)
My Lord,   *Constantinople, January* 14, 1856
I have the honour to enclose herewith, for such use as your Lordship may please to make of them, a state-

ment, drawn up by Brigadier-General Mansfield [Enclosure 2], and an abstract, compiled by Count Pisani, from my correspondence, exhibiting together the series of incidents which have taken place between the Turkish authorities, Her Majesty's Embassy, and the British Commissioner at Kars, from the autumn of 1854 [Enclosure 1].

These papers did not originate with me. I have not even looked through the abstract. General Mansfield and Count Pisani both felt of their own accord that public, and even parliamentary attention might be turned upon the matters in question; that erroneous or exaggerated impressions might possibly be entertained in England as well as elsewhere, and that by setting forth the facts in a clear and concise narrative, they might serve the cause of truth, and afford some eventual assistance to your Lordship's office.

So marked a testimony of good feeling and right-mindedness from persons who are intimately acquainted with all my proceedings on the subject referred to, is naturally gratifying to me, as chief of the Embassy, by Her Majesty's gracious indulgence. I cannot doubt that it will give them a fresh title to your Lordship's esteem.

It is unnecessary for me to fill up the only *lacuna* [missing part] which appears in either the statement or the abstract. I am content to leave the circumstances which are there passed over, to your Lordship's recollection and sense of justice.

STRATFORD DE REDCLIFFE

Enclosure 1

Abstract of correspondence [of Lord Stratford de Redcliffe] respecting the relief of Kars

FIRST EPOCH

From the arrival of General Williams to the departure of Vassif Pasha [August 1854 to January 1855]

August 15, 1854 Arrival of Colonel Williams. He is to go to the Crimea to communicate with Lord Raglan.

August 20, 1854 The town of Byazid is occupied by a Russian force. The Turkish troops in position there are stated to have fled on the approach of the enemy. The great commercial road between Turkey and Persia is thus placed at the mercy of the Russians. A battle has also taken place between the Turks and the Russians in that quarter: the loss very heavy and almost equal on both sides, but the Russians had remained in possession of the field of battle.

August 25, 1854 The more correct statements of the battle of Koorook-Dereh, which have recently arrived, represent the losses of the Turks as more considerable than they were at first believed to be.

I have had some conversation with Reshid Pasha and the Seraskier as to the means of repairing these losses, and I am assured that the Porte may be able to send a reinforcement of 15,000 men to Kars before the close of the season, and 10,000 more in the spring. It is the Porte's intention to place Ismail Pasha in command of the army at Kars, and Mustafa Pasha is preparing to take the command of the smaller army at Batoom, where disease is thinning its ranks to a frightful degree.

September 5, 1854   The most urgent want of the army at Kars at this moment is a Commander-in-chief. The Grand Vizier sent me word that Ismail Pasha was to take the command at Kars.

September 27, 1854   Ismail Pasha, who was lately appointed to the command of it, has been taken ill here. His complaint is an inflammation of the eyes, which may endanger his sight. A provisional Commander, by name Shukri Pasha, is appointed in consequence, with the rank of General of Division. To me the individual and his name are alike new. He is said to have been strongly recommended by Omer Pasha, and also by Ismail, to whom, when with the army, he is to act as Chef d'Etat-Major, superseding in that capacity General Guyon, and having as second in command a certain Hussein Pasha, who is stated to have been serving with Omer Pasha as General of Brigade. The arrival of those two officers at Kars will be followed by the departure of Mustafa Zarif Pasha, Kerim Pasha, and other superior officers, including General Guyon, for Constantinople, when they will be submitted to a Court of Inquiry.

It may be hoped that General Williams, who probably reached the army some days ago, will soon be able to throw a clearer light on its real state, its merits, its wants, and its prospects.

October 4, 1854 Immediately on the receipt of General Williams' despatches, I addressed an instruction to Mr Pisani for the purpose of bringing without delay the wants of the army at Kars to the knowledge of the Porte, and accelerating the transmission of the enumerated articles of supply, including specie, to the army at Kars.

Mr Pisani appears to have found no difficulty in obtaining the assent of the Turkish Ministers to my urgent recommendations, and I am led to hope that there will be no want of exertion on their part. He informs me on the part of the Grand Vizier and the Seraskier that orders for supplying the army with fuel and provisions had been transmitted to the Pasha of Erzeroom; that supplies of grain were to be furnished from Diarbekir, Sivas, Amasia, and the neighbourhood of Erzeroom; that 30,000 sets of winter clothing had been ordered, two-thirds of which had actually been forwarded, and that the rest would follow in a day or two; that 30,000 pairs of shoes and boots, and a similar number of worsted stockings, together with caps and linen, for the soldiers, were on their way to Trebizond; that a number of saddles, tents, and a certain quantity of ammunition had also been sent; that surgical instruments and medicines were ready for shipment; and finally, that 5,000 purses in specie were preparing for transmission to Erzeroom towards the pay of the soldiers.

October 14, 1854   I have much satisfaction in forwarding the clear and able reports of General Williams, who, on reaching the army of Kars, put himself at once into communication with the Commander-in-chief, and took his measures to obtain information calculated to afford a just presumption of the state of things in that neighbourhood.

In one respect I take upon myself to anticipate your instructions. I have already recommended strongly to the Seraskier's attention those improvements or objects of supply which were suggested by General Williams in his correspondence from Erzeroom, and I shall lose no time in pressing upon the Sultan's Government at large the urgent importance of giving immediate effect to those which figure in his subsequent despatch from Kars.

November 15, 1854   Feeling the importance of affording to General Williams all practicable support in the fulfilment of his arduous duties, I applied to Reshid Pasha that the military rank of Ferik, equivalent to General of Division, may be conferred upon that meritorious officer, and I am happy to say that I have His Majesty's authority, communicated to me through Mr Pisani, for informing your Lordship that my request will be complied with.

Agreeably, moreover, to your Lordship's suggestion, the new Commander-in-chief of the army of Kars will be directed to listen to such advice as General Williams may have occasion to offer.

Knowing the extreme importance which your Lordship attaches to the re-instatement of the Turkish army at Kars, I make no apology for transmitting the papers enclosed herewith, which I drew up myself from General Williams' voluminous despatches, and submitted to the Turkish Ministers with an instruction to Mr Pisani, recommending the whole of that officer's demands and suggestions to their most serious and immediate attention.

Later portions of the same correspondence have been conveyed in a similar form and with similar recommendations to the Seraskier Pasha and his colleagues.

I am assured that on the side of the Turkish Ministers there is every appearance of a sincere intention to comply with my demands; as soon as I am satisfied that the supplies are actually sent, and orders corresponding with General Williams' suggestions issued in strongest terms, I shall not fail to apprise your Lordship of so gratifying a result.

The subject being now relieved of much superfluous and exaggerated matter, the course is made clearer to Turkish apprehension, and I trust that the experience of last year, which certainly was painful enough in its most reduced proportions, will have the effect in contributing to the success of my endeavours, grounded on the strenuous exertions of General Williams, and aided by the pecuniary supplies derived from the Loan.

November 29, 1854   In obedience to your Lordship's instructions, I have demanded the trial and punishment of Mustafa Zarif Pasha, the late Commander-in-chief of the Turkish army at Kars. He arrived here a few days ago. I have suspended, meanwhile, a demand for the trials of the Generals of Division, Kerim and Veli Pashas, on account of the altered manner in which General Williams has spoken of the former in his latest despatches. It is desirable to know whether the appearance of amendment continues and extends. I have not, however, neglected the opportunity of remonstrating against the delays which have characterised the trial of Ahmed Pasha and Ali Ferik. I thought it necessary to give my complaint a formal character, by putting it into the shape of an official note. The Ottoman Secretary of State, after having perused it, said that the two last-mentioned criminals laboured under such manifest proofs of guilt that they could not possibly escape.

December 14, 1854   It will be satisfactory to know that some apparent progress is being made towards an improved state of things in what regards the Turkish army at Kars.

An intention has been entertained of sending Mustafa Pasha, Mushir commanding at Batoom, to take provisionally the chief command in place of Ismail Pasha, who is destined to command the army of the Danube during Omer Pasha's absence in the Crimea; but Vassif Pasha, late Commander-in-chief of the Arabian corps d'armée, being at liberty, it is intended to employ him for that purpose.

He will be instructed to attend to the advice offered to him by General Williams, and he will be also empowered to remove, if necessary, Shukri and Hussein Pashas, of whom General Williams has had occasion to complain. Letters of reprimand have been already addressed to those officers, at the same time that letters of approbation have been sent to Kerim and Hafiz Pashas, according to my application founded on the request of General Williams.

December 21, 1854   Among the despatches which I forward from General Williams by the present occasion is one which complains in no measured terms of my silence towards him, and supposed neglect of the interests committed to his care by Her Majesty's Government.

I have time at this moment only to remark that if the charge be correct, my reports to your Lordship must be a tissue of mis-statements. Silent, it is true, I have been, in so far as my correspondence with him is concerned, for the simple reason of my wishing to avoid any risk of disappointment arising out of the dilatory and sometimes illusive proceedings of this Government. But to what degree and with what success I have laboured for the accomplishment of those objects which General Williams has so properly pointed out and so strongly recommended, I hope to place in a clearer light on the departure of the next messenger.

The late Commander-in-chief of the Sultan's army of Kars, Mustafa Zarif Pasha, is placed under arrest, at my requisition, preparatory to an inquiry into his conduct.

His two predecessors are still awaiting their sentence in confinement. The illness of the President of the Council, who is not expected to live, has delayed the procedure.

I have not ceased to point out the necessity of following their conviction with example of condign punishment.

December 28, 1854   I think myself entitled to remark on the hasty manner in which General Williams has allowed himself to suppose that I have neglected the important interests committed to his charge. Because he did not hear from me as soon or as frequently as he expected, he rushed to the conclusion that I gave him no support, and under this inconsiderate impression he has made a deliberate appeal to your Lordship and Lord Raglan.

These circumstances do not in the least degree warp my judgment as to General Williams' excellent intentions and zealous exertions on behalf of the army at Kars, nor am I at all inclined to depreciate the somewhat voluminous correspondence which contains the result of his researches and remonstrances.

Your Lordship is already aware of the pains which I took on the receipt of his principal despatches to put their substance into a working shape, and to engage the Turkish Ministers to enter both promptly and fully on the correction of the abuses which he had denounced.

It is incumbent on me now to show that so far as official assurances go, I have succeeded in obtaining their assent to his leading suggestions, and in some instances a positive execution of the engagements thus contracted.

In order to place my conduct in a true light, independently of my own assertion, I have addressed a set of queries to Mr Pisani, by whose agency my representations, grounded on those of General Williams, have been urged on the Porte, requiring that he should give a distinct reply to each of them, according to the exact state of the case as known to him.

I have certainly to regret that the progress of the Turkish Ministers in acting on my suggestions has not kept pace with the desire of General Williams, nor, indeed, I must say, with those requirements of the service which they concern. But winter, distance, roads scarcely passable, want of funds, the extent of evil to be cured, the scarcity of trustworthy officers, the greater interest of operations elsewhere, the illness of Ismail Pasha, all these causes of difficulty, and others which might be enumerated, have concurred to produce hesitation and delay. I regret the existence of such obstacles, and blame the Turkish Ministers for not surmounting them with more activity. But can I wonder? No; corruption, ignorance, prejudice, want of public spirit, and the instincts of selfishness, engender the same consequences wherever they prevail in long habitual exuberance. The real cause of the culpable inattention shown last year to the wants of the army in Asia is, I learn on authority on which I can rely, the jealousy entertained by the late Seraskier Mehmed Ali Pasha of Mehemed Rouchdi Pasha, at one time his colleague, and at another threatening to become his successor. Unhappily this is by no means a solitary instance. The present Seraskier and Omer Pasha have long been at variance with each other; mutual accusations take place; and while the Seraskier asserts that he has sent ample supplies to the army of Roumelia, the Generalissimo complains of being neglected, and all is contradiction and uncertainty, except one painful fact, the suffering of the soldiers.

If my silence towards General Williams contin-ued longer than I intended, it originated in my anxiety not to occasion disappointment by announc-ing measures which might or might not be carried into effect. I knew that during the winter season lit-tle comparatively could be done, and I preferred, under the pressure of business flowing in abundantly from other sources, to give my correspondent an answer in full, rather than keep up a succession of partial communications.

December 31, 1854   Enclosed is copy of despatch to General Williams forwarding to him the Sultan's fir-man raising him to the rank of a General of Division in the Turkish service.

The list of articles of supply prepared for the army at Kars, or already transmitted thither, as I have received it from the Seraskier, is reserved for a future opportunity in consequence of the difficulty which has been experienced in translating some of the terms which are little known in ordinary composition.

January 11, 1855   I was visited the day before yesterday by Vassif Pasha, who has undertaken the charge of the army at Kars. I recommended General Williams to his confidence and attention in the most unreserved terms, and I endeavoured to impress upon his mind the importance of his acting in cordial concert with that officer, if he wished to render the army efficient, and to meet the views of Her Majesty's Government, identified as they were with those of the Sultan and the Porte. The assurances with which he replied to my injunctions were quite satisfactory, and I hope that his conduct will be such as to redeem the pledge which they conveyed. He spoke of the deficiencies existing in the War Department, and I am under an impression that further exertions will be necessary to have him properly instructed, and promptly sent forward to his destination. I have already expressed myself with earnestness to Reshid Pasha on this subject, and I hope that my words have not fallen on a barren soil. His Highness assured me that Shukri Pasha shall be recalled; that proper deference shall be paid to General Williams, as Her Majesty's Commissioner; and that a Council shall be formed at the War Department to assist the Seraskier, and to give a more steady and efficient direction to his operations.

SECOND EPOCH

From the departure of Vassif Pasha to the commencement of the siege [January to July 1855]

January 29, 1855   I forward herewith three documents calculated to throw light upon the conduct of the Ottoman War Department with respect to the army at Kars, and the points recommended by me for immediate adoption at the suggestion of General Williams. One of them is a report from the Council of the Seraskier's office to the head of that department. The second is an instruction addressed by the Seraskier, Riza Pasha, to the new Commander-in-chief *ad interim*, who embarked from Trebizond a few days ago. The third is an instruction addressed by the Grand Vizier to the same Commander, with the intention of supplying deficiencies in the former.

In pursuance of my instructions, Mr Pisani waited on Vassif Pasha on the 26th. His Excellency gave him positive assurances that he would attend to my recommendations to the best of his ability, and expressed a hope that General Williams would have reason to be satisfied with his exertions to put the army at Kars on an efficient and respectable footing.

Vassif Pasha embarked on the afternoon of the 26th on board the English steamer "London" for Trebizond.

January 31, 1855   The superintendence of the medical hospitals belonging to the Sultan's army at Kars has already been conferred, at my request, on

Dr Sandwith, recommended by General Williams, whose requests with respect to Baron Schwartzenburg, alias Emin Bey, and Tashiar Bey, were also complied with some time ago.

February 5, 1855   I am informed by Her Majesty's Vice-Consul at Trebizond that Vassif Pasha, the new Commander-in-chief of the army at Kars, had arrived there on the 30th ultimo.

Mr Stevens states that the same vessel which conveyed Vassif Pasha to Trebizond had a large lot of military stores, chiefly for winter use, as also 220,000*l.* in specie and paper money for the use of the army.

March 21, 1855   Shukri Pasha, together with Hussein Pasha, has been arrested by order of Vassif Pasha; and the two accused Generals are now, it is to be presumed, on their way to Constantinople for trial.

Mr Pisani informs me that the Seraskier, on hearing of their arrest, declared his conviction that they had been arrested on insufficient grounds, and that he should think it his duty to send in a protest against the measure to the Porte.

Whatever may have been the demerits of the two accused Pashas since their arrival at Kars, they served with distinction under Omer Pasha; and in consequence of the latter's recommendation, had marks of approval and honour conferred on them.

April 16, 1855   Her Majesty's Commissioner to the army at Kars complains of the quarantine at Toprah-

Kaleh being still maintained, in spite of my assurances to the contrary; I have also reason to complain of the delay. The explanation is contained in the accompanying report from Mr Pisani, who assures me that stringent orders have been issued again for its suppression.

The Porte has decided upon the removal of the veteran Mushir, Ismail Pasha, from Erzeroom. The Sultan's sanction remains to be obtained.

April 24, 1855 I have lost no time in acquainting the Porte with the desire entertained by Her Majesty's Government, that any reinforcements which can be spared from other more urgent services should be sent to the army of Kars. I shall take an early opportunity to inform your Lordship of the result of my application, which comes in support of my preceding instances with the weight derived from your Lordship's instructions in the name of Her Majesty's Government.

April 30, 1855 The enclosed report from Mr Pisani informs me that having communicated my instructions to the Turkish Ministers, he was told in reply that they are perfectly alive to the urgency of reinforcing the army of Kars, and that their Commanders repeatedly recommend that measure, but that it is utterly impossible, at least for the present, to spare any of the troops in actual service on the Danube, or in the Crimea.

May 17, 1855   It appears that neither of the two Pashas, Hussein and Shukri, sent down by Vassif Pasha from Erzeroom, on charges exhibited against them by General Williams, has yet been submitted to any legal sentence or judicial proceeding. The former has been applied for by Omer Pasha, as an officer distinguished heretofore by his good qualities, and thought to be capable of rendering good service under the orders of the Commander-in-chief.

On learning this intention, I sent a complaint to the Seraskier, and required that both the Pashas in question should be tried, or submitted to a legal inquiry, on the charges preferred against them. His answer having been less satisfactory than I thought myself entitled to expect, I renewed my application.

May 21, 1855   In reply to further representations in favour of General Williams' demands:

1. The Seraskier reminds me, through Mr Pisani, that the further supplies of the articles of provisions specified in the General's reports, have been forwarded to the army of Kars by the provinces.
2. That the old Ismail Pasha, Mushir of Erzeroom, has been removed.
3. That the Defterdar of that army has been superseded.
4. That orders to the Commander-in-chief to keep General Williams informed of the movements of the troops, and to take his advice, have been given to Vassif Pasha in writing and verbally.

5. That supplies of ammunition were forwarded in sailing vessels by the Ordnance Department more than two months ago.

6. That instructions were sent to Vassif Pasha for the removal and punishment of Injeh Arap and Hassan Yazidgi.

7. That further supplies of money (18,000 purses, or 9,000,000 piastres) have been sent for paying the arrears due to the army, and that more supplies of money are to be sent by the newly appointed Defterdar.

8. The Seraskier added, that he is aware of the necessity of taking into prompt consideration the requirements of the army, but that the state of the Porte's finances cannot allow her to act with the promptitude required.

9. That Salih Bey is not dismissed.

10. That camels are not to be got, but that the purchase of mules is in progress, and orders for the preparation of arabas have also been given.

11. That out of the 1,000 gunners required by General Williams, 400 have already reached Kars, and the remainder are to follow forthwith.

12. That the other matters recommended by General Williams in his report of February 18, to me, have been attended to, as proved by the Seraskier's report to Fuad Pasha, communicated to me by the latter.

June 14, 1855 I have again pressed the trial of Hussein and Shukri Pashas. The Seraskier contends that the charges brought against them have nothing to do with the service, and that they are purely personal quarrels. He also promises to answer me in writing, stating at the same time that Omer Pasha bitterly complains of the neglect shown by his predecessor in his omission to send Hussein Pasha to the Crimea, and insists upon having him there without loss of time; therefore that the Seraskier cannot refuse compliance with Omer Pasha's demand without incurring some responsibility.

The latest advices from General Williams intimate that the Russian movements at Gumri manifested an intention to attack the Turkish army at Kars. I had previously renewed my applications to the Porte, and urged the Turkish Ministers to send up further supplies and reinforcements if possible, even at this late hour. I most particularly urged the importance of forwarding a considerable sum of money without delay. The Seraskier asserted in answer, that some of the supplies forwarded by his predecessor had been acknowledged by the Acting Commander-in-chief. He added, that the larger portion of what had been required from his office had been transmitted, and that he was preparing to transmit the remainder by the earliest steamer. He admitted that according to the latest intelligence, the Russians appeared to be coming down in force.

June 15, 1855   On the receipt of a despatch from General Williams, informing me that appearances warranted an expectation that the Russian forces at

Gumri were meditating an attack upon Kars, I lost no time in communicating with the Porte and the Seraskier, repeating my urgent remonstrances that reinforcements, with fresh supplies and money, should be sent out forthwith to Kars.

June 20, 1855   I went over to the Porte yesterday, and saw the Kaimakam, Fuad Pasha, and the Seraskier, who, with much civility, left the Council Chamber, where they were deliberating on the means of reinforcing the army at Kars, and afforded me an opportunity of again recommending to them in person, the urgent importance of making up for past delays by sending succour of every kind to that army with all practicable dispatch. These gentlemen had every appearance of entering fully into my views, and I trust that no time will be lost in carrying their intentions, late as they are, into effect. The Seraskier expressed a decided opinion that a body of 10,000 men might be detached from Batoom without danger to that establishment, which still has 4,000 or 5,000 for its protection. It was proposed, at the same time, that some vessels of war should be directed to cruise along the coast of Circassia; and I was requested to submit this plan to Rear-Admiral Sir E. Lyons, under an impression that a joint operation, in concert with the French, would be desirable.

The Turkish Ministers are under an impression that the position occupied by the Army at Kars would not enable it to withstand a vigorous attack on the part of the Russians, and that if the enemy appears in force Vassif Pasha will probably have to fall back on Erzeroom.

June 25, 1855   Enclosed herewith in translation, is an official memorandum addressed to me by the Porte, with reference to the charges brought against Shukri and Hussein Pashas by General Williams. After the representations which I had previously made to the Porte in support of General Williams' complaints, it would be useless for me to prolong the discussion without instructions from Her Majesty's Government. On the whole, I think it preferable to bring under your Lordship's unbiased judgment the excuses and arguments offered by the Porte. There is nothing in the meantime to prevent my informing Fuad Pasha that such is the course which I intend to pursue, and to submit to his cooler consideration the propriety of suspending any definite act of acquittal on behalf of the accused Pashas, until I can be put in possession of your Lordship's opinion.

June 28, 1855   Advices from Trebizond, which came round to me through Lord Raglan, describe the Russians from Gumri as being within a few days' march of Kars. Their force is stated at 36,000, a number which considerably exceeds the previous estimate. The Turkish forces, including all between Kars and Erzeroom, with the circumjacent stations, cannot safely be carried beyond an amount of 20,000, if so much, and the Seraskier has prepared me for a retrograde movement on their part, it being his declared opinion that the positions at Kars are not tenable against the enemy.

His Excellency and his colleagues are naturally desirous that no time should be lost in counteracting the Russian attack; and it is some consolation to me to find that even at this eleventh hour the necessity of listening to my advice and sending off reinforcements without further delay is recognised.

But where are reinforcements to be found in sufficient quantity? How are they to be provided with necessary supplies? What plan of operations offers the best chance of employing their service with efficiency?

Nothing can with prudence or consistency be detached from the army under Omer Pasha in the Crimea. At Batoom, Soukoum-Kaleh, and other neighbouring stations on the coast, it would be extremely difficult to muster more than 11,000 men, though a higher figure was quoted at first.

In Bulgaria I question the existence of more than 50,000 men, including garrisons. The other parts of the Empire afford no additional resources, with the exception of Bosnia, where it is still possible that a few thousand men might be detached. I speak of Regulars. Bashi-Bozouks may be procured; but your Lordship knows what little dependence is to be placed on such undisciplined hordes. There remains the half-formed corps of General Vivian, and the Irregular Cavalry of General Beatson, incompletely organised.

June 30, 1855   A meeting took place this morning at the Grand Vizier's house. In addition to his Highness, the Seraskier and Fuad Pasha were present. I was accompanied by Brigadier-General Mansfield.

We found that the Porte had received advices from Vassif Pasha, brought by an officer who had left Kars about eleven days before. Despatches from General Williams also came to hand at the moment we were entering into conference. Their latest date was the 19th instant.

It appears from both sources that the Russians advancing from Gumri with an amount of force varying from 20,000 to 30,000, had presented themselves before Kars; that a partial engagement of Cavalry had taken place, followed two days later an attack, which had been repulsed, on the part of the enemy, and that the town was threatened with a siege.

I collected from the Turkish officer that when he left the scene of action rain was falling in torrents, the waters of the river were out, and the Russians had no choice but to encamp. It appears from the English statements that the defences of the fortress were deemed to be of considerable strength, that the place was provisioned for a month, and that the Turkish army may be calculated at 18,000 men.

It was clear to all present that, whether the Russians besieged or turned Kars, the Turkish army required the effort to be made for its relief with all practicable dispatch, and that of those possible modes of acting for that purpose, the only one likely to prove effective was an expedition by Kutais into Georgia.

To send reinforcements by Trebizond would be, at best, a palliative. To establish an entrenched camp at Redoute-Kaleh, as formerly proposed by the Porte, would, at this unhealthy season, be equivalent to consigning the troops to destruction.

The real question was, whether a force numerically sufficient, and in all respects effective, could be collected in time at Kutais to make an incursion into Georgia and threaten the communications of the Russian army, placing it, indeed, between two hostile forces, should the Turkish army still be in a condition to take the field.

It was for the Turkish Ministers to solve this problem, and they proposed that the expeditionary force should be composed of 12,000 men from Batoom and the neighbouring stations, of the troops made over to General Vivian, and estimated at 10,000 of all arms, of General Beatson's Irregular Cavalry, of 10,000 men to be detached from the army in Bulgaria, as the complement of the Turkish Contingent, of 5,000 more derived from the same source, of an Egyptian Regiment of Horse, and of another regiment, expected from Tunis. To these the Seraskier proposed to add 2,000 Albanians by way of riflemen. These several forces, completed according to the figures, would furnish a total of 44,400 men, but perhaps to be reckoned with prudence, at not more than 36,000 effective.

Admitting the urgency of the case, and the consequent necessity of incurring a certain degree of hazard, I called attention to the importance of not exposing the Turkish Contingent or General Beatson's Horse prematurely to a trial beyond their strength. It was accordingly understood that, supposing the expedition to be resolved, neither of these corps would be required to embark for Redoute-Kaleh until the preparations were completed in other respects, and it is to be hoped that the interval thus gained for their benefit would suffice to secure their efficiency. I took, moreover, the liberty of remarking that the proposed expedition, besides being prepared with secrecy, and sanctioned by supreme authority, must finally depend for its adoption on our available means of providing it with all the requisite appliances. This indispensable field of inquiry might be investigated, with advantage, by General Vivian, the Seraskier Pasha, and General Mansfield, who, indeed, have undertaken to meet tomorrow for that purpose.

The Turkish Ministers having expressed their readiness to entrust the direction of the expedition, should it eventually take place, to a British Commander, and to accept General Vivian in that capacity, subject, of course, to the approval of Her Majesty's Government, I lost no time, after our separation, in communicating personally with that officer, and putting him in possession of all that had passed on the subject of our discussion.

July 6, 1855　The Seraskier informs me that most of the articles demanded for the army of Kars had been actually forwarded, and that more were preparing, and that 600 Artillerymen, besides those already sent, were preparing to embark with a large supply of ammunition.

July 12, 1855   The extreme importance of obtaining correct data before the expedition proposed for the relief of Kars be finally submitted to Her Majesty's Government, produces an unavoidable delay in the progress and preparation of the plan. The Porte has decided on sending confidential officers to examine the localities at Trebizond, Batoom, and Redoute-Kaleh, with a view of forming a more correct idea of their resources and difficulties. I hope that General Vivian and Sir E. Lyons will pursue the same course, and that an officer from each service will be sent in a suitable vessel to obtain the requisite information on the coast. I have already applied to General Vivian and Rear-Admiral Grey for that purpose, and I shall avail myself of the earliest opportunity to make a similar application to Admiral Sir E. Lyons.

On the same 12th July, the following telegraphic message was transmitted to the Earl of Clarendon:

> Preparations for an eventual expedition are in progress. It might save much valuable time if you would inform me at once by telegraph whether the Government is prepared to sanction a powerful diversion by Redoute-Kaleh and Kutais into Georgia, if local investigation and the engagement of Turkish and allied authorities as to the means of execution should warrant a calculation of success.

THIRD EPOCH
During the siege [July 1855]

July 16, 1855   On the night of the 14th instant I received despatches to the 2nd from Kars and Erzeroom. It results from their contents that Kars was surrounded by the Russians, who had established themselves on the high road leading to Erzeroom; that the garrison of the latter place was very weak, and that a portion of the provisions collected for the army was cut off; but that the troops and garrisons were in good heart, and to all appearance resolved on a foil performance of their duty.

With the view of ascertaining how far the advices received by the Seraskier from the same quarters corresponded with those addressed to me, and what real progress was being made in the preparation of measures calculated to operate in support of the beleaguered army, I requested General Mansfield to call upon that Minister. I am now informed, as the result of that interview, that the advices received by the Seraskier, though of the same date, and similar for the most part in substance to those received by me, are on the whole of a more encouraging character than the latter. They add to their confirmation of the resolute attitude assumed by the Ottoman troops at Kars, an assurance that the subsistence of the army was secured for three months; that 500 Irregulars had thrown themselves into Kars; that 300 artillerymen, with 20 guns, since followed by 500 from the Dardanelles and here, were on their way to the scene of action; that Hussein Pasha of Trebizond had taken the same direction, at the head of 10,000 Irregulars, and that plenty of ammunition was collected at Erzeroom.

It further appears from the Seraskier's statement to General Mansfield, that the inhabitants of Erzeroom had summoned the Pasha on his own responsibility to hasten to the assistance of Kars, and that he had in consequence assembled a body of Irregulars, and marched in that direction, without waiting for orders from Constantinople.

Another body of Irregulars, to the amount of 4,000, is to be raised by Toussoum Pasha, himself in former times a Bashi-Bozouk, and directed from Sivas into the country around Kars, with a view of controlling the operations of the Russian Cossacks in that quarter.

When General Mansfield expressed, in conversing with the Seraskier, his apprehensions as to the dangers of employing a numerous horde of Bashi-Bozouks, collected on the spur of the occasion, and probably ill-provided with everything, his Excellency replied that he had insisted on having the necessary funds wherewith to pay them, which was the main instrument of control, and that he had threatened to retire from office if his demand were not complied with.

With reference to the eventual diversion into Georgia, the Seraskier informed General Mansfield that the plan had been communicated to Omer Pasha, whose answer, however, had not yet reached his hands; that the 15,000 men in Bulgaria, destined to form part of the expedition, were in readiness to march to the coast with sufficient means of transport, and that, in general, his preparations were so far advanced as only to require the assent of Her Majesty's Government to be carried into practical effect.

July 19, 1855   Omer Pasha, apprised by the Seraskier of the danger to which Kars was exposed, and also of the plan for relieving it, which was under consideration here, had proposed to withdraw from the Crimea the 25,000 Turkish troops before Sebastopol, and to put himself at their head in order to operate a diversion from the coast in Circassia. Not finding among the English and French Commanders-in-chief any disposition to support him, he announced his intention of proceeding at once to Constantinople, with the view of submitting his opinions to his Government. He arrived here the night before last.

This impulsive resolution is by no means in keeping with the decided opposition offered by Omer Pasha to the late Seraskier's requisition for detaching 5,000 of his men for the Crimea. His Highness may account for the change of view by referring to the pressure at Kars, and to the suspension of active operations before Sebastopol. But the Generals, his colleagues, deprecate the latter ground of justification, and means might apparently be employed for the rescue of Kars without deranging the calculations of the allied armies in the Crimea.

Your Lordship is already acquainted with the plan which has been for some time under consideration here on the part of the Sultan's Government, in concert with Her Majesty's Embassy. An appeal has, moreover, been made by means of the electric telegraph to Her Majesty's Government, who were entreated to lose no time in making known its pleasure to the proposed diversion, supposing it to obtain the suffrages of the naval and military authorities in point of means for carrying it into effect. The answer may be expected from day to day, and a final decision may then be taken, with the advice and concurrence of the Commander-in-chief. It would have been idle to make any earlier communication to them of an official description: the state of the army at Kars was made known to the British Commander-in-chief by General Williams himself.

I have this day received the following telegraphic message from your Lordship:

> The plan of operations for reinforcing the army at Kars, contained in your Excellency's despatch of the 1st July, is disapproved. The reasons will be sent by the messenger today against employing the Turkish Contingent until it is fit for service.
>
> Trebizond ought to be the base of operations, and if the Turkish army of Kars and Erzeroom cannot hold out at the latter place against the Russians, it might be proper to fall back on Trebizond. It would easily be reinforced.

July 30, 1855   The unfavourable judgment passed by Her Majesty's Government on the plans which have been lately under discussion, with a view to the relief of Kars, has naturally increased the Porte's embarrassment. It was my duty to make it known to the Turkish Ministers, not only as an opinion, but, with respect to General Vivian's Contingent, as a veto. Her Majesty's Government not only withhold the Contingent, but express a decided preference for the alternative of sending reinforcements to Erzeroom by way of Trebizond. This opinion is not adopted by the Porte, or indeed by any official or personal authority here. The Seraskier, Omer Pasha, General Guyon, and our own officers, as far as I have means of knowing, agree with the Porte and the French Embassy in pressing a diversion on the side of Redoute-Kaleh, as offering the better chance of success, supposing, of course, that the necessary means of transport, supply, and other indispensable wants can be sufficiently provided. France is, at the same time, decidedly adverse to any diminution of force in the Crimea; and Omer Pasha, ready to place himself at the head of an Asiatic expedition, requires for that purpose a part of the troops now there.

Such being the present state of the case, I am precluded from contributing to the Porte's extrication from its difficulties, otherwise than by countenancing some new location of the Contingent, which without exposing the corps to a premature trial, might enable a force of the same amount to be detached for service elsewhere.

No final decision has yet been taken by the Porte. The French Ambassador has written for General Pélissier's opinion, and Omer Pasha is still in attendance on his Government.

Meanwhile the advices from Kars are not encouraging, and time, of precious value, is unavoidably wasted in doubt and uncertainty.

Enclosure 2

Memorandum by Brigadier-General Mansfield on the measures taken for the relief of Kars since his arrival at Constantinople

On the 26th of June, or about a week after my arrival at Constantinople, I visited the Seraskier Pasha by the desire of Her Majesty's Ambassador. The subject discussed was the relief of the army at Kars.

Two plans were talked over. The one being the march of a force from Trebizond, which would have been necessarily collected from various distant points. The second being the formation of a camp at Redoute-Kaleh, with the intention of making a strong diversion for the relief of Vassif Pasha by real menace of Georgia. A few days afterwards there was a meeting at the house of Aali Pasha, the Grand Vizier, at which were present his Excellency Lord Stratford, Fuad Pasha, the Seraskier Pasha, Mr Pisani (the head Dragoman), and myself.

The meeting was very secret. We sat for five hours in Council. The Redoute-Kaleh project was seriously discussed. It was proposed by the Turks to employ the

Contingent, giving the chief command of the expedition to General Vivian.

The Turks were very confident of being able to find the necessary means, and there seemed to be general unanimity in the prudence of the Redoute-Kaleh project, if it were carried out at once. It was argued that the dispatch of slender reinforcements by way of Trebizond and Erzeroom would not only not effect the object, but would expose the people so employed to be cut off in detail.

That there was reason for this argument was shown by the after-movement of Mouravieff to Kupri-Keuy, the garrison of Kars being masked by 15 battalions left in position and a large body of Cavalry.

It was proposed, in consequence of the meagre Russian resources in Mingrelia, to land 20,000 men at Redoute-Kaleh, throw them boldly forward on Kutais, the remainder of the army to follow, as it could be gathered together from various quarters.

The strength of the entire force available for the campaign was estimated at about 44,000 men, with guns and horses in proportion. His Excellency having the greatest anxiety to relieve the besieged garrison, was in constant communication with the Porte. I was, on more than one occasion, dispatched to discuss the matter with the Seraskier Pasha. The project was formally communicated to General Vivian, who was requested to propose estimates of means required for the expedition.

That officer accompanied me to the Seraskierat early in July, and in my presence thanked the Seraskier

Pasha for the honour conferred on him by the Government of the Sultan in the offer of the chief command. On the 9th of July I attended at a meeting of all the Ministers at the house of Fuad Pasha, when the details of the contemplated expedition were most carefully examined as regards men, material, provisions, land and sea transport.

By his Excellency's request, Major-General Smith was sent to reconnoitre Redoute-Kaleh and the neighbouring coast; and a report was also received from Captain the Honourable — Drummond, of Her Majesty's ship "Tribune", on the same subject. I have reason to believe that the movement of troops in Bulgaria towards Varna for shipment, was ordered at the same time by the Turkish Government, that is to say, that they were held in readiness, the whole scheme having been fully referred by the Ambassador to Her Majesty's Government for consideration. Various circumstances with which I have no concern, conspired to arrest the progress of the undertaking.

General Vivian did not consider his force ready for active service; Omer Pasha arrived suddenly from the Crimea; there was a disinclination to part with any troops from that quarter, and apparently an equal one to substitute for a portion of them the embodied regiments of the Turkish Contingent.

During this time urgent letters were constantly in course of arrival from General Williams and Vassif Pasha. It was alleged that the garrison could not hold out for more than two months. During the time lost its affairs were becoming more straightened, and we soon learnt that the daily ration was reduced. The well-appointed and numerous Russian Cavalry swept the whole country on a radius of twelve hours' march from Kars, and every magazine in the neighbourhood was cleared of its contents.

The Ambassador never ceased from making the most urgent representations to the Seraskier and the Porte. On the receipt of every fresh despatch from Kars and Erzeroom, either Mr Pisani or myself was sent to enforce the necessity of relief. My appearance at the Seraskierat might indeed have been considered an ill omen for the garrison of Kars, so frequently was I obliged to make the same representation. As may be seen from my numerous reports of the last four or five months, there was no want of alacrity on the part of the Turkish Government. There was a dilemma from which they sought to extricate themselves, but in vain. They could only accomplish reinforcements by driblets to the garrison of Erzeroom, and they were thwarted by the apathy of their own commanders.

If I may be allowed to offer an opinion on the real cause of the disastrous issue of the Turco-Asiatic campaign, I should say that it must be found in the nature of the alliance, which absorbed all the really available means of action, whether French, British, or Turkish, in the invasion of the Russian soil, to the exclusion of attention to the hostile operation on Turkish territory. The contest pursued in the former required every practicable means to ensure success, perhaps, may be said, even military safety.

The garrison of Kars performed a great duty in arresting the march of the Russian columns till the resources of the allies could be turned to Asia, either in consequence of a development they had not already reached, or of liberation from the Crimea.

Some months since I ventured to predict, in private conversation, that we should have to be satisfied with such an issue of the operations of the last year; and that, assuming the allies to be prepared to take advantage of what has been thus achieved by the devoted garrison, we should have no reason to be disappointed when viewing the two theatres of war as one comprehensive whole. I have no reason to depart from the opinion then expressed.

With regard to the proceedings of the Embassy, I may be permitted to add, that after a disposition was shown to enable Omer Pasha to go to Asia, no effort was spared to expedite his movements; and that if events had marched with the same rapidity as the wishes of his Excellency, we possibly might not now have to lament the surrender of Kars.

W. R. MANSFIELD,
Brigadier-General

Consul Brant to the Earl of Clarendon
(received February 7)

My Lord,   *Erzeroom, January* 15, 1856

I have the honour to transmit to your Lordship, copy of a despatch which I have just addressed to Viscount Stratford de Redcliffe. I wrote it as an act of justice to

Tahir Pasha, and to prevent his being made the scape-goat of Selim Pasha, who is infinitely more culpable. Tahir is, like all Turks, apathetic, but he is far superior to most in intelligence and honesty, and I hope he will not be allowed to be thus unworthily sacrificed.

JAS. BRANT

Enclosure

Consul Brant to Lord Stratford de Redcliffe

(Extract)   *Erzeroom, January* 15, 1856

I have the honour to inform your Excellency that it is intended, at the Porte, to make Tahir Pasha the victim to cover the fault of those who, in reality, caused the fall of Kars, and I must, in justice, denounce this plot of the Seraskier Pasha's, as I believe it to be, to screen Selim Pasha from punishment.

It is pretended that, last winter, Tahir Pasha did not introduce stores into Kars, but I can state that the fault was not Tahir Pasha's, it was that of Shukri Pasha, the then President of the Medjlis, who lowered the carriage so much that no carrier would take grain to Kars at the rate offered. As soon as Shukri Pasha was removed, Tahir Pasha took his post, and immediately raised the carriage, and supplies were sent. That Tahir Pasha was energetic, and did all that might have been done, I will not pretend; but I assert that he did more than any other member of the Medjlis, and is certainly the least culpable of all the Pashas.

The Earl of Clarendon to Lord Stratford de Redcliffe

My Lord,   *Foreign Office, January* 21, 1856

In reply to your Excellency's despatch of the 31st of December, I have to acquaint you that Her Majesty's Government have learnt with satisfaction that you have obtained a promise from the Porte that Mehemet and Selim Pashas shall be forthwith removed from their respective commands at Erzeroom.

CLARENDON

Lord Stratford de Redcliffe to the Earl of Clarendon
(received February 6)

My Lord,   *Constantinople, January* 24, 1856

I have sent Fuad Pasha an extract of your Lordship's instruction of the 10th instant, respecting the misconduct of Selim and Tahir Pashas.

The Seraskier told me yesterday that he believed the former of those two Pashas to be innocent, and he stated some particulars in support of his opinion. As the accused General is to come away from Erzeroom, and as an inquiry will be instituted into his proceedings, I thought it useless to repeat the charges which stand against him.

With respect to the deficiency of supplies, the blame is thrown upon a deceased Commissary, who had the position of Defterdar, and whose son has been thrown into confinement as an accomplice, to answer for the alleged malversation.

STRATFORD DE REDCLIFFE

At the close of these despatches, in January 1856, the main combatants of the Crimean War were poised to make peace. Final negotiations were agreed in March 1856 in Paris. The Treaty of Paris, however, which affirmed the integrity of the Turkish Empire, was to prove as futile as the war which had preceded it.

Other titles in the series

The Amritsar Massacre: General Dyer in the Punjab, 1919

"We feel that General Dyer, by adopting an inhuman and un-British method of dealing with subjects of His Majesty the King-Emperor, has done great disservice to the interest of British rule in India. This aspect it was not possible for the people of the mentality of General Dyer to realise."

Backdrop

At the time of the events described, India was under British rule. Indians had fought alongside the British in World War I, and had made tremendous financial contributions to the British war effort. Mahatma Gandhi was the leader of the Indian National Congress party, which was seeking independence from the British Empire.

The Book

This is the story of the action taken by Brigadier-General Dyer at Amritsar in the Punjab in 1919. Faced with insurrection in support of Mahatma Gandhi, the British Army attempted to restore order. General Dyer, on arriving in the troubled city of Amritsar, issued an order banning any assembly of more than four people. Consequently, when he discovered a large crowd gathered together during a cattle fair, he took the astonishing action of shooting more than three hundred unarmed people. Regarding the subsequent native obedience as a satisfactory result, he was surprised to find himself removed from command a year later, and made lengthy representations to Parliament.

ISBN 0 11 702412 0   Price £6.99

British Battles of World War I, 1914–15

"The effect of these poisonous gases was so virulent as to render the whole of the line held by the French Division incapable of any action at all. It was at first impossible for anyone to realise what had actually happened. The smoke and fumes hid everything from sight, and hundreds of men were thrown into a comatose or dying condition, and within an hour the whole position had to be abandoned, together with about 50 guns."

Backdrop
On 4 August 1914, Britain declared war on Germany. Germany had already invaded Belgium and France and was progressing towards Paris.

The Book
These are the despatches from some of the battles of the first two years of World War I. They include action in northern France, Germany, Gallipoli, and even as far afield as the Cocos Islands in the Indian Ocean. They describe the events of battle, the tremendous courage, the huge losses, and the confusions and difficulties of war. These startling accounts, which were written by the generals at the front, were first published in the "London Gazette", the official newspaper of Parliament.

ISBN 0 11 702447 3   Price £6.99

Florence Nightingale and the Crimea, 1854–55

"By an oversight, no candles were included among the stores brought to the Crimea. Lamps and wicks were brought but not oil. These omissions were not supplied until after possession had been taken of Balaklava, and the purveyor had an opportunity of purchasing candles and oil from the shipping and the dealers in the town."

Backdrop

The British Army arrived in the Crimea in 1854, ill-equipped to fight a war in the depths of a Russian winter.

The Book

The hospital service for wounded soldiers during the Crimean War was very poor and became the subject of concern, not just in the army, but also in the press. "The Times" was publishing letters from the families of soldiers describing the appalling conditions. This embarrassed the government, but even more it irritated the army, which did not know how to cope with such open scrutiny of its activities.

The book is a collection of extracts from government papers published in 1855 and 1856. Their selection provides a snapshot of events at that time. In particular they focus on the terrible disaster that was the Charge of the Light Brigade, and the inadequate provisions that were made for the care of the sick and wounded. The documents relating to the hospitals at Scutari include evidence from Florence Nightingale herself.

ISBN 0 11 702425 2   Price £6.99

Lord Kitchener and Winston Churchill: The Dardanelles Commission Part I, 1914–15

"The naval attack on the Narrows was never resumed. It is difficult to understand why the War Council did not meet between 19th March and 14th May. The failure of the naval attack showed the necessity of abandoning the plan of forcing the passage of the Dardanelles by purely naval operation. The War Council should then have met and considered the future policy to be pursued."

Backdrop

The Dardanelles formed part of the main southern shipping route to Russia, and was of great military and strategic importance. However, it had long been recognised by the British naval and military authorities that any attack on the Dardanelles would be an operation fraught with great difficulties.

The Book

During the early stages of World War I, Russia made a plea to her allies to make a demonstration against the Turks. So attractive was the prize of the Dardanelles to the British generals, notably Lord Kitchener, that this ill-fated campaign was launched. Just how powerful an influence Kitchener was to exert over the War Council, and just how ill-prepared the Allies were to conduct such an attack, are revealed in dramatic detail in the report of this Commission.

The book covers the first part of the Commission's report. It deals with the origin, inception and conduct of operations in the Dardanelles from the beginning of the war in August 1914 until March 1915, when the idea of a purely naval attack was abandoned.

ISBN 0 11 702423 6   Price £6.99

The Russian Revolution, 1917

"It is the general opinion in Ekaterinburg that the Empress, her son, and four daughters were not murdered, but were despatched on the 17th July to the north or the west. The story that they were burnt in a house seems to be an exaggeration of the fact that in a wood outside the town was found a heap of ashes, apparently the result of burning a considerable amount of clothing. At the bottom of the ashes was a diamond, and, as one of the Grand Duchesses is said to have sewn a diamond into the lining of her cloak, it is supposed that the clothes of the Imperial family were burnt there."

Backdrop
By November 1917 Russia had lost more than twenty million people in the war. Lenin's Bolshevik party had overthrown the Tsar and had called for an end to all capitalist governments.

The Book
Government files contain a number of detailed documents describing the nature of the Bolshevik Revolution and the government of Lenin, which was observed to be not only abhorrent but also menacing because of the international implications. The book is compiled from two of these files, one of which describes the events leading up to the revolution and how the Bolsheviks came to power in October 1917. The other contains a series of eye-witness accounts of the frightening days of the Bolshevik regime from the summer of 1918 to April 1919.

ISBN 0 11 702424 4   Price £6.99

UFOs in the House of Lords, 1979

"Is it not time that Her Majesty's Government informed our people of what they know about UFOs? The UFOs have been coming in increasing numbers for 30 years since the war, and I think it is time our people were told the truth. We have not been invaded from outer space. Most incidents have not been hostile. Indeed it is us, the earthlings, who have fired on them. . . . Whatever the truth is, I am sure that an informed public is a prepared one. Another thing: it is on record that both sighting and landing reports are increasing all the time. Just suppose the 'ufonauts' decided to make mass landings tomorrow in this country—there could well be panic here, because our people have not been prepared."

Backdrop
The winter of 1978/79 in Britain was a time of strikes and unrest. It became known as the "winter of discontent". Yet it seems that the House of Lords had other more important things to discuss.

The Book
The book is the transcript of a debate in the House of Lords which took place in February 1979. Their Lordships debated the need for an international initiative in response to the problem of Unidentified Flying Objects. There were several notable speeches from noble lords and distinguished prelates.

ISBN 0 11 702413 9   Price £6.99

D Day to VE Day: General Eisenhower's Report, 1944–45

"During the spring of 1945, as the sky grew darker over Germany, the Nazi leaders had struggled desperately, by every means in their power, to whip their people into a last supreme effort to stave off defeat, hoping against hope that it would be possible, if only they could hold out long enough, to save the day by dividing the Allies. Blinded as they were by their own terror and hatred of 'Bolshevism', they were incapable of understanding the strength of the bond of common interest existing between Britain, the United States and the Soviet Union."

Backdrop

In 1944 the Allies were poised to launch an attack against Hitler's German war machine. The planning and timing were crucial. In February, General Eisenhower was appointed Supreme Commander of the Allied Operations in Europe.

The Book

The book is Dwight D. Eisenhower's personal account of the Allied invasion of Europe, from the preparations for the D-Day landings in Normandy, France, to the final assault across Germany. He presents a story of a far more arduous struggle than is commonly portrayed against an enemy whose tenacity he admired and whose skills he feared. It is a tactical account of his understanding of enemy manoeuvres, and his attempts to counter their actions. The formality of the report is coloured by many personal touches, and the reader senses Eisenhower's growing determination to complete the task. Hindsight would have had the general take more notice of Russian activity, but that this was not obvious to him is one of the fascinations of such a contemporary document.

ISBN 0 11 702451 1   Price £6.99